SHADES OF
BLACK 'N' BLUE

by

Stephen Hayes

Grosvenor House
Publishing Limited

All rights reserved
Copyright © Stephen Hayes, 2022

The right of Stephen Hayes to be identified as the author of this
work has been asserted by him in accordance with Section 78
of the Copyright, Designs and Patents Act 1988

The book cover picture is copyright to Stephen Hayes

This book is published by
Grosvenor House Publishing Ltd
28-30 High Street, Guildford, Surrey, GU1 3EL.
www.grosvenorhousepublishing.co.uk

This book is sold subject to the conditions that it shall not, by way of
trade or otherwise, be lent, resold, hired out or otherwise circulated
without the author's or publisher's prior consent in any form of binding or
cover other than that in which it is published and
without a similar condition including this condition being imposed
on the subsequent purchaser.

A CIP record for this book
is available from the British Library

ISBN 978-1-83975-988-8

Introduction

In history 2012 and 2013 will go down as the years which exploded so many myths about the honesty of the police. There were astonishing revelations, including the unbelievable Hillsborough conspiracy, Jimmy Savile, Bryn Estyn Children's Home, the Cyril Smith MP investigation, the miners' strike report and finally the Andrew Mitchell Plebgate affair. All high profile and all with one common theme, a deep-seated culture within the British police that they honestly believed that they could write anything, however fictitious, and be believed.

Surely these high profile examples must only scratch the surface of what is repeatedly being revealed with regular monotony in the media as a corrupt culture within the police. Moving on into the present century I opened a Twitter account to run with the initial book, The Biggest Gang in Britain.

The book was advertised and a website opened www.thebiggestganginbritain.com offering other members of the public the opportunity to share their 'police' experiences. Before embarking on this public relations exercise I believed I had been badly victimized by the police with regard to a couple of matters. I can honestly say that my knowledge based on my years of police service and personal experiences having left the force actually pale into insignificance. There are many other examples on Google, so many that it is often unbelievable. There are almost endless demonstrations of police corruption in differing forms, ruining the lives of countless individuals: for example just search Ian Puddick on Google and stand back. This man is not a nutter, he has a successful plumbing business. His only offence was for his wife to have an affair with a City of London businessman who had friends in the police and as a result he stirred things up a little to draw attention to this man and various police practices. It is an amazing read. For a wider and fully informed summary of police dishonesty and failings in their many interpretations go to Jean James website and register your interest for her mailing list. It is truly incredible.

As I have repeated so many times, such incidents are not of a rogue element involving a few corrupt individuals, but a deep and ingrained culture in every force. Of course it is to varying degrees, fermented over years with the help of 'head in the sand' politicians, refusing to act and publicize the many police failings. MPs have so many skeletons, which clearly continue to proliferate, and these only came to the public gaze with the MPs' expenses scandal. There was clearly a reluctance to prosecute, but in appeasing the public unrest they were forced to press charges and did so with only a couple of blatantly criminal examples, who in turn received only minimal prison sentences which were further reduced with the so-called tagging system, now itself totally discredited. So many other potential prosecutions were quickly swept away, many more without any further mentions, or prosecutions. Meanwhile, Joe Public continues to be prosecuted and imprisoned on the flimsiest of fabricated evidence on numerous occasions.

With such an ever-increasing background of very dubious incidents, how can the regularly reported fall in crime figures be believed? Even the hysterical Police Federation has appeared in the media, complaining of these blatant fabrications. The forces involved are generally county forces covering large areas throughout the UK. Forces, which have always had a reputation for failure and sheep-shagging rather than real police work. Such large areas are no longer effectively policed due to the savage cuts in police personnel with more to follow. Small sub-stations have been closed, probably now boutique restaurants. The communications centres are now centralized, covering these massive areas, staffed by civilians with no local knowledge and inevitably a bad attitude. The public is talking with their fingers, they have had enough, they are not reporting petty crime, they are not prepared to dial 999 and wait in excess of 30 minutes for a half-hearted response. In so many areas throughout the UK a pizza is baked and delivered quicker than police respond to an emergency. Crime figures have not fallen, they have not been recorded, and the public has ceased to talk to the police on so many levels. Crime is continuing as it always has, it is probably on the increase due to the economic crisis, but a very disillusioned public who just do not know where to turn for support is not reporting the crimes.

Just as simple examples; how can Nottinghamshire Police show a drop of 21.7%, Northumbria 17.6% and West Midlands 13.6%? How can a typical police constable spend only an average of eight minutes in every hour on the beat and produce such dramatic figures as an average 10% drop has taken place in reported crime? The simple answer is that they can't, it is impossible and once again the ingrained culture of written deceit and lies within the police throughout the UK is fooling the media and Government alike.

How can a Government naively take genuine comfort from such figures and feel vindicated by the cuts with more to come when it suits and realistically we must ask whether they actually know or at least suspect the truth, but again do not wish to upset the biggest gang in case further skeletons in the MPs' cupboards appear. They are still reeling from having to instigate the Hillsborough conspiracy investigation in the same year and what will inevitably prove to be a half-hearted whitewash, sorry investigation into that disgraceful conspiracy, Plebgate and so many more.

David Cameron in a Sky News interview recently stated that 'The police are relatively honest.' Look under Stephen Hayes The Biggest Gang In Britain at my You Tube rendition of this un-researched and ludicrous statement – aren't they supposed to be honest? Not just relatively honest? The figures only go to prove that the public really are losing faith in the police and are now recognizing that, at the wounded heart of all examples is a culture of fabricated reporting, deceit and lies.

In addition to the fabricated reports prepared by the police on the miners' strike in the summer of 1984, a multitude of arrested miners were found not guilty by a disillusioned Joe Public in the form of the 'twelve men, good and true' of the jury. They based their decisions on the many suspect prosecutions supported by so much perjured police evidence. Let us not be fooled by empty claims "that was then" and today all is well and above criticism. Only recently in Culcheth, rural Cheshire, members of the Greater Manchester force shot dead an unarmed car driver said to be conspiring to commit an armed robbery with three other men. The evidence proved to be so flawed against what were known to be active criminals that a jury found them all not guilty, clearly again as a public protest to such corrupt evidence, despite the men concerned being well known to the police.

For so many years the police have relied upon a jury to have what they regarded as commonsense and convict whatever the flawed evidence, believing without question the evidence put before them. But no, the wheel is coming off in regular and dramatic style. However, despite the cracks appearing, how long will it actually be before the police themselves are prosecuted and convicted for perjury in relation to the many examples of fabricated evidence which abound with such regular monotony today? Will the Hillsborough conspiracy be the first?

What has happened to the police of today? Untrained and amateurishly they try to emulate our working practices of the 60s and 70s. The difficulties arise because they don't have the expertise to choose their deserving targets and the verbals, cock-ups and perjury, which were commonplace are now being questioned by the disillusioned public. Today they have just had enough and are voting accordingly in such public displays. Is it really surprising when with recent humiliation they were proved to be Plebs the title they objected so strongly about and even then were unable to successfully 'cock-up' a cycling MP?

The police of today are so badly led and with such limited leadership come the obvious inabilities to detect crime in whatever fashion. To compensate for all these inabilities we continue to be yet again subjected to statistical manipulation at all levels with so many alarming and damaging consequences. Politicians seek to appease the Police Federation, because of the Plebgate affair and the accompanying embarrassment from which all choose to pick and mix the fabricated figures to suit the current need of proving that so many frontline redundancies are having no effect. It is a pity that they didn't consult the Police Federation before such a statement was issued, because they do not agree and also claim the figures to be fabricated.

So onward and upward, as the wheels of justice continue to grind with Her Majesty's finest at the pointed end. Not necessarily risking life and limb except for the very rare serious assault on an officer. These fill the TV news and the papers for a day and are then forgotten and it's back to the everyday big issues of dieting, X Factor, I'm A Celebrity and of course the ever present bent Members of Parliament, yet to be found out but always suspected. Even when eventually caught with their hands in the till they are allowed to wriggle out of any real prosecution. The troops (police) at large continue in their gang-like manner, trying to earn a few quid by fair means or foul, cocking up the evidence, verballing and generally inflicting the 'Enid Blytons' on anyone silly enough to deny the reason for arrest whether justified or not. However the wheel is turning and the unending trust is waning.

Where did it all start?

Let us return to 1829 when the Metropolitan Police started from such humble beginnings and rigid ideas to the unsupervised and badly led shambles we have today.

ROBERT PEEL

My thoughts drift to the early days of the police for comparisons and Sir Robert Peel (1788-1850). Of course, with such illustrious beginnings I have to wonder how far the quality of recruited men and their supervising officers in today's police forces will have to free fall before any drastic action is taken and a total rethink of all aspects is treated as a priority.

Known affectionately as Bobby, Sir Robert Peel founded 'The Peelers' - what is now the Metropolitan Police - whilst he was the Home Secretary in Lord Liverpool's Tory Cabinet.

Prior to this the UK was a lawless conglomeration of crime-ridden towns and cities, much as today, having apparently gone the full circle. We are clearly in need of a strong Home Secretary as the resulting police leadership on the ground is laughable. This of course, has been the case for many years and more recently we've enjoyed the form of female Home Secretaries promoted to the position, with no experience of life, only to admit in various forms that they had no idea of what they were doing, having no experience at all in running what is effectively a big business.

Compare and contrast them if you will to Sir Robert, who successfully built the Royal Irish Constabulary in 1812, then confidently built his second new force having passed the Metropolitan Police Act in 1829.

The initial 1,000 men were all dressed in blue tailcoats and top hats and equipped with a truncheon and handcuffs and a wooden rattle to call assistance, which was later replaced with a whistle. The uniform was chosen to differ from the army uniform of red and to blend more into the public way of dress. The Peelers were governed by strict rules. They had to be 6ft tall. They worked seven days a week with only five unpaid days holiday per annum for the princely sum of £1 per week. To prevent public suspicion of being spied upon they wore the uniform whether on or off duty. Their lives were controlled to the point of them being barred from voting, requiring permission to marry and being prevented from dining with a civilian.

From these charming and humble beginnings has evolved the police force of today, the Biggest Gang in Great Britain and through the years since then, the average police officer has 'raped' and 'pillaged' his way through the unsuspecting public with a level of dishonesty and corruption unthought-of by founder Sir Robert. And by and large this self-serving behaviour with little thought for law and order has been totally disbelieved through the ages by the ever adoring public. Despite so many distasteful incidents there are still many millions who want to innocently believe the content of Dixon of Dock Green, Heartbeat and latterly The Bill. The rose-coloured glasses are clouding and the public are slowly recognizing the fact that today's police force consists of a scruffy short-arsed rabble very rarely venturing from the safety of their motor vehicle unless accompanied by at least one colleague. And up to the same old tricks as back in my time but without the expertise to avoid detection.

There are so many laughable incidents appearing with unnerving regularity, such as the pensioner being Tasered for carrying a white stick which the half-wit police officer believed to be a Samurai sword, the CS gassing of a good Samaritan assisting in detaining a criminal, the arrest and detention in a cell of a farmer and his mother protecting their property and so many more. Of course these are the tragic incidents which again only prove the failings in training and supervision emanating from the root cause of senior officers with no experience and therefore the inability to pass on any practical and relevant knowledge. Officers have died in firearms training, the shocking instance of two female Greater Manchester Police officers, who were allowed to visit a suspected crime scene in an area where a dangerous fugitive was known to be, a fugitive who had boasted he was keen 'to kill a copper.' Before the atrocity Greater Manchester Police had played to the media, showing off their helicopters, their armed response units, the saturation coverage of the area and yet these two women were allowed to continue without any support with the tragic consequences that shocked the nation. And their colleagues must have been absolutely appalled that it was allowed to happen – I've spoken to pals still in GMP and they were sickened by the lack of proper supervision and joined up thinking that could have prevented this tragedy. The senior officer in command of this shambles has now been moved from that division.

As such events have illustrated, the police are out of control. They are badly trained, badly led and poorly selected in the first place. From men of real presence and stature, in the days of Sir Robert, through to the generation I now write about. These are often cowards in uniform, who are now small men with all the hang ups associated with men of minimal stature and authority, as they strut along our streets, craving respect, yet failing miserably.

A man 5'6" tall which is the minimum in several forces, adorned in all the accoutrements associated with police authority of today, the essential stab vest, de rigeur telescopic truncheon, handcuffs, tear gas or CS, radio, mobile telephone, not forgetting the Taser and all this topped with an ill-fitting flat cap and high visibility jacket which certainly does not attract any public respect.

With equality came the policewomen. Initially formed in 1917 in Manchester, but without full police powers and it was only in 1940 that WPCs were given powers to assist with the war effort. Today from such humble beginnings they are all decked out with the same equipment, shorter still but expected to perform the same duties despite having the appearance of a kissogram in the case of the rare attractive ones and generally attracting the poor levels of respect one would expect.

It is through such ranks that the promoted senior officers climb. They have spent all their few years of service hiding from real police work, sometimes out of fear, sometimes total incompetence, but always gaining little experience, spending most of their service in administration jobs to facilitate their attendance at various universities and police training establishments. Having been promoted through the ranks they are expected to lead by example and thereby lies the problem and the reasons for such lack of control.

Of course, the success of any business relies on the 'man/woman at the helm' and down the ladder through his various supervisory officers. Success thereafter depends on the experience and capabilities of the chosen 'leaders.' A police force is no different. Where it differs from business is the fact that it does not have to show a profit to survive, merely produce statistics which hopefully prove at least some element of hard work and proper guidance. Statistics are an art and the detection rate can be fabricated and only since real detectives have been replaced by university graduates has the detection rate fallen dramatically. The honest detection rate has always been abysmal and has always relied on informants and fabricated TICs (offences taken into consideration) as I will relate in some detail later.

In my day the drinking, pillaging and shagging always had to be curtailed occasionally in case it prevented any real police work on too much of a permanent basis. Having had a brief history lesson, a profound and honest comparison, perhaps helping to reduce the already natural disgust and surprise, read on.

Of course in highlighting such failings, what I say is difficult to believe. Even Andrew Mitchell MP of Plebgate fame was quoted as saying that his faith in the police is not, shall we say, what it was before they stitched him up like a kipper. There are now numerous newspaper articles highlighting the many police failings with this particular incident only proving to be a humorous diversion, but with a deep and unsettling message. Mr Mitchell was a member of Her Majesty's Government and yet uniformed constables, basically put on the simple duty of 'gate guarding' and clearly regarded as unsuitable for real police work had the gall to fabricate evidence against such a figure, again in the confident knowledge that they were fireproof in avoiding any real discipline procedures in a culture which has protected the police generally for so many years. Only now, with a serving MP suffering a simple attack of the 'Enid Blytons' has the entire corrupt and accepted practice of fabricating evidence to suit come to the fore. This incident has focused all the country's attention on what must be recognized as a lot more than just a rogue element of an illustrious police force. It is quite sad to note that the internet is bulging with so many examples of police corruption through various websites such as Ian Puddick, Patrick Cullinane, Jean James, Police Stop and so many more and yet it takes an incident of pantomime proportions to raise the public interest.

It is after all simply a few men merely continuing with an accepted culture that has rotted the innards of the police for many years on a nationwide basis. However, on this occasion it all had such dire consequences for the police, which in the real world should lead to many prosecutions, especially of the 'old school' senior ranks who are still living in yesteryear in permitting such stitch-ups to occur.

Yet back to the sunny 70s and 80s when things were looking up for yours truly or perhaps I was being hidden away by the increasing populace of weak and unqualified senior ranks where I could do little damage and continue to ridicule their obvious failings.

A DYING DECLARATION AND A VERY DIFFICULT TIME

THE BODY was found, a needle beside him, the usual junkie overdose. Only this one had left a little note: 'I have not killed myself, Hayes has done this. He thought I was dead but I have been able to write this.'

Now that would be funny as a final joke, but it wasn't going to get laughed off easily and it most certainly wasn't a gag. They say revenge is a dish best served cold, well the body was very cold indeed and nobody could put a time of death on it as we'd then had a warm snap encouraging the inevitable decomposition. But that scrawled message was a dying declaration and taken very seriously. It carried a great deal of evidential weight. It was a legal document and very worthy of belief, in the desperate circumstances of such a death.

First I knew about it was when I got arrested. It's not the phrase you want to hear as a policeman: 'Anything you say may be taken down and used in evidence against you.' Now don't get me wrong I didn't like the Scottish chap who had died, but I wouldn't be able to give him an overdose without leaving any evidence at all at the scene, or inflicting some marks that would have been picked up in the post mortem. I might have given him a good slap and had in the past, but that was because he was a thieving junkie who preyed on pensioners and terrorized the elderly in pursuit of his next fix.

With the time of death not accurately assessed due to the existing level of decomposition I could not give a strong alibi for the lengthy period involved in the doctor's assessment. Having said that, there was nothing to indicate I had done anything. The syringe by the body was checked for fingerprints and the only one on it was the victim's. The Drug Squad's general use of the giant syringe to extract confessions, seeking an alternative to the wet towel, didn't help my denials and even gave the note some credibility. Surprisingly, I was not suspended, as I would have been today, even If I had been accused of stealing an orange.

The "powers" didn't take the claim seriously. It was the days of police versus shitheads and there was only one winner, whatever the circumstances. This was similar thinking to that employed in the preparation of the Hillsborough reports. No one would believe the police could be at fault, so why aggravate the situation with a 'little truth.' They allocated my investigation to Chief Superintendent Coyle. A strange decision for what could be a murder charge and it certainly confirmed in my mind that they also believed that the note was not regarded as genuine or serious and, perhaps if it was, the means justified the end. Little Mr Coyle had the appearance of an "Alice in Wonderland mole" – peering out from behind his spectacles. He was not a detective. He had probably never seen an angry man. He was not a policeman, full stop. He was in charge of the force administration, salaries, sickness, and most of headquarters' other paper-pushing duties.

The appointment pleased me greatly. There was a lot I could read into it - exoneration for one. The report was immaculate and well typed, but everyone with any experience knew it would come to nothing. My star informant came to the nick, which was unusual. He had blown his cover to tell me that he had been drinking with a relative of the victim who had bought a gun. The relative wanted to procure my home address, was offering a large sum of money and intended to kill a member of my family. My star informant believed the threat and if he did, then so did I. Without hesitation I informed my superior, Detective Inspector Eric Jones, who took the unprecedented step of requesting an armed policewoman to escort my wife when shopping. He allowed me all the time at home I needed and I had to tell my wife not to leave the children outside for fresh air, despite the good weather. My daughter was a toddler, but my son still slept incessantly between feeds and still does for that matter.

It was a difficult time and I always had someone with me. They wouldn't allow me to be armed as they were aware of the consequences. There was absolutely no doubt that I would have shot anyone who threatened my family in this way or even if I thought they would. I was fully prepared to take any action whatever was involved. On one occasion a colleague and I were on Deansgate in Manchester when I realized we were being followed by a family member of the deceased, as we headed for the Manchester Crown Court building.

We led the individual into the court building and upstairs into the corridors of offices. We were able to grab him, establish he wasn't armed, and push him into the nearest room which proved to be the barristers' robing room. We gave him a serious good hiding without a visible bruise and all this in front of the learned counsel who never uttered a word. We dragged him out onto the street with a further strong caution. Despite this conclusion to such an incident, still, further attempts were made later to follow me by other members of this family. I was constantly being kept up to date with local information and from the feedback these scrotes believed they had me spooked and were taking considerable pleasure from the situation. I went to Coyle and informed him of the situation. His lack of credible police thinking and the miserable office boy outlook on life ensured that he failed to accept the potential seriousness of the situation and told me I was a police officer and no one would attack me. I then went to see Charlie Horan the Detective Chief Superintendent head of CID for the entire force. He was a real policeman; he had many solved murders to his credit and a history of service at 'the pointed end' throughout his career and grasped the situation immediately.

Some weeks before, these unsettling incidents, the IRA had blown up a coach on the M62, killing many soldiers seated at the rear of the coach. The soldiers had all boarded at Chorlton St bus station in the city centre. Before they did so, all the luggage had been piled at the rear awaiting loading into the luggage compartments. Security was abysmal in those days and it was a simple matter for the IRA to add a bag containing 25lbs of explosives to the pile. The investigation was coming to a conclusion. A Stockport lady called Judith Ward was fitted up by all accounts for the nine dead soldiers and three civilians – well she served 18 years before being released on the grounds her IRA bombing convictions were unsafe. The Irish police through real police work and their network of informants had identified some of the culprits and discovered that they had returned to the province. There was little more the squad could do and Charlie Horan put them all on sorting my problem. The deceased prisoner's family was based in Oldham, but some were traced to Scotland. One was stopped on the Forth Bridge. They knew that we were aware of their activities and had been left in no doubt and in some considerable pain. This was the police protecting its own at its very best. The Biggest Gang in the form that it should operate had come to the fore. This was officers, some of whom who had never met me, doing what came naturally in a 'there but for the grace of God' climate. The internal inquiry on me and the post-mortem had been completed. The coroner directed a verdict of suicide and even commented that the suggestion of murder was nonsense. The matter was officially closed.

But it didn't stop. When we moved to our new house, my wife had dealt with the fitting of the phone and in the nice little world in which she existed never knew of ex-directory numbers. They were not so widely used as today and the number appeared in the directory before I realized. I received a call, asking for me. It was not threatening, it was not particularly suspicious. For no other reason than instinct, alarm bells rang and I knew instinctively what the call was about. My voices warned me in the strange indescribable manner I have enjoyed, all my life. I denied any knowledge of Stephen Hayes, but couldn't really tell if I was believed. There was nothing more the job could do and realistically, it was left to me. By then I was capable of anything. I was totally capable of committing murder to protect my family. I suppose everyone says this, but in my case it was true. Before I could get myself in deeper, one of my best friends in the force and who will remain anonymous for the purposes of this little story had called in an enormous favour from a serious professional hard man. This is a man who was to appear in the newspapers some months after, being wanted for armed robbery. If I gave all the fantastic details he would be immediately identified and I still owe him much.

When Charlie Horan pulled me in to his office, he was mildly concerned and had an air of disbelief. The family lived in a terraced house in Oldham. The front door had been kicked off the hinges whilst the Horlicks was being sipped during yet another peaceful evening in front of the TV. I was informed that the lounge ceiling had been blasted with a pump-action sawn-off shotgun until the legs of the shredded bed in the room above protruded through the joists. The terrified family, with the now blanched appearance of the Horlicks they were drinking, were made to be silent and pay attention to the warning of future action of a "more serious nature" should their attention on me continue.

I told Charlie the truth. I had no idea this was to happen or who was responsible and, indeed, this was the truth, I had no idea who would pull off such a stunt, though I was extremely grateful to whoever it was. Charlie let a glimmer of a smile cross his face. He said: "I can't have this Dodge City behaviour. You will get into serious trouble. I want you to calm down and leave Didsbury. Go to the Regional Crime Squad. Don't do anything. Sit back and just calm down."

It was to be the beginning of the end of my police career and the dead man was just another junkie scumbag. How I came to know him was purely by chance as smashed out of his head he started robbing little old ladies. We had this nasty spate of thefts from pensioners in Didsbury. They were not simple sneak-ins, but a male pushing a frail old lady back into the house and frightening her into revealing the locations of cash. Even under such duress they were canny enough to deny any knowledge of jewellery, inevitably antique, passed down the generations and of some value.

The culprit had been described on several occasions as tall, with long hair, purple trousers, and looking like a hippy. The offences were continuing on a daily basis all over the division, but the man was never apprehended despite his fashion sense and the purple trousers. He was committing these brazen offences in broad daylight and yet never appeared in our sights as we criss-crossed the section in our cars and even as a desperate measure, actually on foot. Detectives never walked. I called in Dave, the trusty informant, who had built-in radar and he actually had him located within 24 hours - his name, his address and the fact he was a registered drug addict. Without doubt this was all the proof necessary of the value in mixing with villains, drinking with them and discussing all the local gossip and yet in the police of today, this is forbidden. With the address, we gave him some serious attention. We would follow him from home, again resorting to actual walking, provided it wasn't raining of course, as he staggered through the back streets and entries, oblivious to our presence and only intent on blagging another little old lady for enough readies to score a deal of drugs. We followed until he committed yet another offence. We didn't wait until he had terrified a lady but in the knowledge that he was about to actually commit some kind of offence we would arrest him. Again fabrication of a few evidential factors would have to be introduced to protect the elderly victim. We believed he had been dissuaded at the nick from committing other offences and despite the bruises, he continued with his criminal activities once out on the streets of Didsbury again. We did this several times and charged him with the offences as we saw them take shape. Of course he didn't know any better as he suffered the withdrawals from his drug-fuelled existence and would have admitted to anything to get out and score again.

He appeared at court, was bailed, and then simply continued to commit offences. The magistrates wouldn't listen to our applications to have him remanded in custody. They could see the previous list of offences was growing and that he was extremely pale and weak. What appeared to be pity allowed them to bail him yet again. The magistrates lived in such a rose-coloured world of distorted reality that they took no account of the distress the pensioners had suffered and yet again due to their failure to grasp reality let him out onto the unsuspecting streets. For elderly people to suffer the knowledge of someone going through their personal effects can be a distress which stays with them for the rest of their life.

We quickly realized that we would have to introduce some more realistic police work into this situation and made this man a priority. We all continued to follow him, catch him before he actually caused any distress and arrested him, adding the points of evidence necessary to ensure the offence. If a door was wide open, it would be closed in evidence and the fact he pushed it open without so much as a knock or a shout would prove his dishonest intent. If a window was open on a hot day, the evidence would be that it was only open a couple of inches and that he had opened it wider to gain entry. Rather than waste the time in attending court with him he was placed on police bail, which meant he was immediately released and free to continue with his burglaries and thieving. We were actually stacking up such a volume of offences that the sentencing allowed by magistrates would be seen as insufficient and the case would have to be taken out of the hands of the magistrates and the villain would have to be committed to the Crown Court.

On what I regarded as the final day of this exercise in law enforcement and public protection, I saw him peering through a side window of a house which adjoined a school playground. The window was open and he climbed inside the house. I ran to the window, looked through, but he had gone from view. I climbed in, tripped, and as I fell into the room, the culprit reappeared and made his way to the window as I was falling through it. Luckily, he broke what could have been an awkward fall, and I had him on the floor as the householder entered the room. There was a mild struggle as I lined him up with a few smart punches and a wrestling hold. Luckily I was able to identify myself before the elderly householder brained me with a walking stick, which he was already raising to deliver a blow.

My new friend wasn't so fortunate and as I struggled to climb to my feet whilst hanging on to him, the pensioner attacked the intruder with his walking stick, with such ferocity that I also suffered a couple of blows. The thief was nicked. Out came the full list of all the offences committed on bail and eventually he appeared at court. My plan had failed as the stupid magistrates quite amazingly made yet another confused decision in relation to his liberty and yet again bailed him until he could appear on the list for his appearance at Crown Court. The general police work was difficult enough without strangely naive magistrates granting unlimited bail to active criminals, so being intent on turning Manchester into a haven for criminals to commit further mayhem.

I never saw him again and couldn't understand why. I continually searched the area, but to no avail. There were no further reports of similar crimes and so we decided he had left the Division and moved on to pensioner pastures new avoiding the heat in Didsbury. Not so and it was only when I was "arrested" that I discovered that the prisoner had committed suicide by injecting himself with a large overdose of barbiturates. Fair enough, a common method chosen by many addicts. They had no idea what they were doing and often failed to crush and dissolve the tablets effectively. The end result was an embolism or similar blocking their already shriveling veins and often resulting in death. With large volumes of the drug, which was usually Mandrax, the end result could be a simple overdose and again death. Not so in this case. My little friend had taken an overdose, deliberately and in doing so he had left a little note. Very inventive and amusing if it was treated as the joke it clearly was, but the start of an amazing set of circumstances.

But I'm rushing ahead of myself, I was on the job – if you'll pardon the expression - for a good bit before this. It was a remarkable journey from the beat to so many different bedrooms and back to day-to-day policing as a detective. The beat goes on and so does my journey through the curious world of cops both uniformed and plain clothed.

Who needs James Bond...never shaken they rarely stir

Whilst in the Drug Squad, we were strangely regarded as part of Special Branch for the reasons I have given in book one The Biggest Gang In Britain. Hard drugs were unheard of in the 60s and 70s in Manchester, but in keeping up with the Jones', in this case the Metropolitan Force and in ticking a couple of apparent efficiency boxes at the Home Office, a Drug Squad was put together. Nobody knew what they were doing, the squad had no officers and so it was put under the control of Special Branch, Manchester's answer to James Bond. This department had a ranking structure, including a Chief Inspector, a couple of Inspectors, Sergeants and all of them were merely a paper exercise to tick further boxes at the Home Office. The IRA was in its infancy and not seen as the threat it grew to be, or at least not seen as any real threat at all in Manchester by this hardy group intent on tracing only illegal immigrants.

In being part of this department we were regarded as the in-house shitheads and then used for what was described as operational matters. In truth, our assistance involved undertaking some of their typically minor enquiries in the evening, when the Special Branch did not work. I always found it strange that a body of men purporting to be James Bond did not work after 5pm and certainly did not go out in the dark. They were effectively Manchester's equivalent of the Gurkhas, in so much as they took no prisoners. Today the Special Branch has more to do, even in Manchester where they are claiming to be involved in monitoring terrorism with the abundance of illegal immigrants on the patch. In London, Scotland Yard has had some considerable successes with the help of MI5 and its' network of informants and undercover operatives, in making the arrests they have to date. Manchester appears to be falling behind in that area, but one hopes they're keeping calm and carrying on as the old wartime saying goes.

Of course, the present day drug scene has totally changed. There are now warring factions of blacks from the Cheetham Hill and Moss Side areas of Manchester. The whites are well into the cocaine, as of course are the blacks. The Chinese are very civilized, as one would expect from their historical roots and generally keep it amongst themselves. They deal very heavily with their own and only come to the fore when an apparently innocent chef is attacked with a machete on his doorstep, having cooked his drug dealing books rather than the Peking Duck.

Today guns are widely used and it is commonplace to see men in their 20s, or even teens and younger, on a mountain bike with a bulletproof waistcoat in Moss Side. To the bystander like me it is apparent that the PC police of the present have totally lost control, despite, I have to say, the valiant efforts of Superintendent Bill Kerr and his army of well-placed informants. Drug Squad officers have often been threatened by the drug gang leaders. The threats are carefully prepared and relatives identified. Many take the easy way out and both the villains and the police alike would buy a villa in Spain with the ill-gotten proceeds of their trade.

Bill Smyth was a good detective in his day and an ex-Drug Squad officer, who later worked for me as my office manager in my first private detective agency. He was threatened by a big wheel drug dealer who had also established the addresses of his sister and mother. 'The Job,' as the police is internally known, couldn't stop it. The difficulty by then was that all or most of the squads were led, and I use the term lightly, by weak officers as described earlier, being inexperienced but with an ability to study for examinations. It appeared to him that even the hierarchy of the police, just did not know or even care about protecting their own. By this time the supervisory ranks were being drawn from the protected circles of accelerated promotion and university degree courses. They were either frightened, or totally out of their depth – or even both, and generally chose the ostrich approach of burying their heads in the sand or more accurately picking up another sheaf of paper to write crimes around. As a result of this total apathy towards his situation Bill resigned, having lost all confidence in his superior officers and the protection 'The Job' offered for the few who were still prepared to stick their necks out. Having moved into the business world I made it my life's work to employ policemen who were forced to leave the service for a variety of reasons, usually emanating from deplorable leadership. I did not employ anyone dismissed for dishonesty, as if they were stupid enough to get caught then they were no use to me. Having worked for me for many years, Bill went his own way intent on starting his own company with a proven lazy shithead who I also once employed, so there was little hope of success. I have not seen him since he left the company.

In Liverpool today, conditions are even worse. Drug trafficking and general gangster activities are blatant. There are many shootings and threats to police, who appear to be led with more confidence than those in Manchester, but clearly still not well enough. In both forces there are many informants to the drug world. Such informants come in all shapes and sizes and surprisingly from all areas of the judicial system, including court staff, who on the face of things appear to be the retired pensioners they are, but beneath this façade is a villain's informant fighting to get out with information on a well-protected search warrant. There is so much corruption, often borne of fear, but usually out of greed, throughout the many forces in the land. Taking a bribe is the easy option, when you have no one in authority to turn to and no guarantee of personal safety if you do. It is a culture which emanates from my early days in the 60s and 70s when the commission of crime was commonplace within the police and apparently condoned by the supervisory ranks.

It was very early in my career that I was taught always to take over the dominant high ground and use whatever tactics came to mind in doing so. During my police service I was prepared to use any weapon at hand and often did. In true Life On Mars style I have assaulted prisoners with a variety of weapons ranging from a bottle, a bar stool, a shop window, flights of stairs, a pair of scissors and even a car. The fact is that the more any detective did then the chance of confrontation will be greater as you make enemies and encounter situations that can get violent in the detection of crime.

Of course, the Special Branch we had in those early days was in its infancy and now I was part of it, however loosely attached. Special Branch to me was not so much The Spy Who Loved Me more the spy who loved himself. I might even have had a licence to kill, but in my case the job was not to fire the gun and shoot anybody - something for which I was trained and often dreamt of. They didn't have such dangerous things to contend with as the Islamic terrorists of today. There were not so many political issues as there seems to be now. Looking back, it is strange to remember that the IRA was little more than a rumour and generally laughed at by these so-called intelligence officers.

One evening we were briefed by Inspector George Dampier, who had been dragged away from his dance class. Gorgeous George, as he was known, kept a pair of patent leather dancing shoes in the Special Branch office. His evening duties generally consisted of sweeping a 'little beauty' off her feet with a dazzling foxtrot at the Ritz dance hall. On this occasion, however, we were to raid a house in the Plymouth Grove area, thought to house a man with IRA connections. Plymouth Grove, close to Longsight Police Station, was a popular area for the Irish labour contingent who resided in Manchester and, indeed, one of the best nights out in the area was the Irish club known as the Carousel.

Gorgeous George was the only man allegedly trained to use a firearm on duty at the time and was there to lead us into the house in his shiny new bulletproof jacket and clutching his Webley revolver. These would have matched his patent leather shoes admirably, had he worn them.

George appeared to be not very keen on the fact he was at the pointed end. Apart from being in grave danger and facing the possibility of being killed he was likely to get blood on his rather fetching floral patterned tie. Leaving the police with a posthumous Queen's Police Medal was not in his plans.

It was quite amusing to watch him as we approached the house. We dived straight in and kicked the door off its' hinges. We were good at that, it was a skill developed in the Drug Squad to prevent the occupants flushing the cannabis and speed down the toilet. Instead of rushing straight in, George stood back, as though marking time in a quick flash of the Gay Gordons. It was obvious this was not what he wished to miss a dance class for. This was a critical time and to maintain the element of surprise, we made an instant decision and ran in before the suspect could stand and act as we believed he would. He was watching TV and never moved. It was hardly surprising, George asked the trembling unfortunate a few questions and from the answers quickly deduced that we were sitting on and strangling the wrong man. Even in those days, so long ago, the Manchester Special Branch still specialized in arresting the wrong person.

Our suspect got a letter of apology, a new door, and probably a pacemaker. George knew we were taking the piss regarding his heroic style and rather than have such a situation occur again he sent some of us on the firearm shooting course. The object was to turn us into sharp shooting police marksmen, so we could be the first to be shot. Supervision from the rear was a trait becoming all too prevalent in the police leadership of the day. We went to an Army firing range, somewhere near to Glossop in Derbyshire, for one day where we were allowed to fire a military type recoilless rifle, which couldn't possibly miss because of the number of bullets per second it fired. This weapon was not issued to the police of the day. It was never used by the police as it is today and the fact we fired it was for novelty value only. The soldiers in charge just enjoyed playing with it to demonstrate what they had for a war.

We were rather disappointingly trained with Webley .38 revolvers, a gun that had the smallest butt possible. An effective grip was difficult for men with large hands as they could not hold the gun firmly. With my tender, lover's fingers of pianist proportions I was better suited to holding the butt. Of course I had held many butts, but most supported above high heels and often enveloped in lace. We all shot about ten rounds at a target some 20 feet away. I hit the target six times. Others didn't hit it at all. As I have said, I was declared a marksman and was to be called on in circumstances where a marksman was necessary or, in truth, they were desperate, very desperate indeed. Unfortunately, they were never that desperate and, to my everlasting disappointment, I never shot anyone. Years earlier on the mobile column we had been instructed to shoot the ring leader in any scenes of public disaffection after a nuclear war. But back in those days we never had any guns, so it was a particularly bizarre instruction – though it did appeal to me and would certainly have been a welcome addition to our armoury of bar stools and tables on a Saturday night in Manchester.

The reference to such an astute body of highly trained marksmen, always evoked thoughts of intense training and a wealth of experience, observing terrorists and any individual likely to cause a threat to the Crown. It is therefore difficult to comprehend how such 'in depth' instruction could evoke the following humiliating episode.

Many years after my valiant service, as I was out in the big wide world, the Manchester Special Branch bristling with training and expertise, probably brought on by increased terrorist activities and the many successes in the efficient Met, arrested four so-called terrorist suspects for having weapons of mass destruction, allegedly to blow up Manchester United Football Club at Old Trafford. In a raid they had found match tickets for an important clash with Liverpool and felt such a find was vital proof of the conspiracy. Such a find was not in retrospect, surprising because they were all long standing Manchester United supporters. The white powder 'explosive' they discovered in the raid when examined in the laboratory, transpired to be something like Daz washing powder. There was no way that even the Special Branch could hide such a result as they had foolishly shouted their 'success' from every Manchester rooftop.

Even with the Hillsborough experience fresh on the horizon and their flawed thinking, they should have realized there was nowhere to hide, the results were publicized particularly in the Manchester Evening News. It must so often have hurt readers seeing the local newspaper publish stories of Manchester police glorification when the truth was so incredibly different. Even this newspaper could not hide from these facts and once again the police were a laughing stock in the eyes of the public.

In such a total public relations failure of laughable proportions they would surely have affected the morale of their colleagues who had to continue in a climate of ridicule particularly amongst the Asians of Manchester. The city in parts is said to be a terrorist hot bed and in turn, this has given the militant Muslims a clear account of their actual capabilities. They have probably also convinced the non-militant Muslims that their intelligence, and use of such information, is so poor that they are at risk if they pass on any information to the authorities.

In the climate of 'No Smoke Without Fire' they must surely have believed that these men were guilty, they must have had other information and therefore rather than cause so much embarrassment, and in the heartfelt traditions of my days, they would have added a little evidence and 'verbals.' There is no doubt that many officers with whom I served would have made sure that traces of explosives in the form of forensic evidence were found in the flat, or would even have fabricated evidence in a manner which would leave no doubt, such as finding a stick of explosive preferred by Al Qaeda in a car or business premises. The fact they were innocent, mattered little. Prisons today have many prisoners serving life sentences regarded as unsuitable for parole purely because they continue to protest their innocence. Nobody considers the fact that they could be yet another example of corrupt and fabricated evidence and purely out of an amazing strength of principle were refusing to bow to this antiquated system.

I was amused, as I often am, to watch Lancashire County Police motorway patrols on a recent television documentary being filmed as they performed their daily duties. Performance is surely the ideal description as they play up to the cameras in their 'wooden' childish way. Surely the viewing public recognized these as the overweight, arrogant, and small-minded shower that is certainly damaging the force nationwide and doing the police image so much harm today, if indeed such assistance was necessary. Such police documentaries are now prolific, they tend to feature smaller county forces which have never been renowned for their policing abilities. All these multitude of programmes have one common denominator. They show the police and the courts as an absolute waste of time. How often do we see youths abusing them in street confrontations and arrests, whilst they progress through the detention system to a point where they are released without any charge or appear at court to receive a minimal sentence. The present TV image of this 'gang' can have done nothing for the men at the real pointed end.

I remember years ago former Home Secretary Michael Howard on the David Frost Sunday Show stating the Tories were not against forming a trading unison with the EU, but did not wish to be obliged to accept every directive from Brussels. He used as an example, the fact that Brussels wanted to bring in random breath tests, but the Tories would resist this and other such policing controls. I liked Michael Howard and would have voted for him, but I would be much happier if he had properly researched his 'soap boxes.' I find it so hard to believe that politicians and the media in general have not recognized, or discovered that random breath tests have operated since the inception of the breathalyser itself. Many drivers have lost their licences based on fabricated evidence relating to their standard of driving, their weaving about the road or even a deliberately broken tail light if it was decided to argue the point. It is a simple matter for the officer to break the light with his truncheon and then give evidence that the car was stopped because of the damaged light. Who would believe a driver's futile protestations that the officer broke the light to give a reason for detention and the use of the breathalyser.

Magistrates in their own little naive world of power are even known to increase a sentence purely because the accused had the temerity to cast doubt on the honesty of the police officer. Such corruption of evidence is common at all levels of offences and of course in some instances necessary to ensure a conviction in cases of much more importance than a trivial traffic offence. The pettiness of actually committing what is after all perjury in relation to a simple traffic offence is a very worrying aspect and once again just goes to prove that even the lowest of the low uniformed officers believe they have the God given right to fabricate evidence at will, whatever the circumstances. A classic example is of course Plebgate, where Andrew Mitchell MP was the alleged victim of fabricated evidence by men who many would recognize as Plebs. Especially by the police themselves who gave them a duty as simple as guarding a gate and they then break the inevitable boredom by stitching up a member of Her Majesty's Government.

The murder detection rate today throughout the country is now, of course, abysmal. The most common murders usually relate to family members or close friendships in a wider group. Only such murders with family connections are now detected and only then because the actual evidence is so blatantly obvious. During the days of the 60s and 70s as I have already written all murders were detected. Whether the accused had actually committed the offence was immaterial.

Today Murder Squads are, at the risk of repeating myself yet again, led by senior ranks with no experience of life, let alone actual detailed detection procedures whilst leading a murder hunt effectively, which should really be based on years of experience. Today senior officers do not gain that experience as they flit from one course to another at various police training establishments and university degree courses. Of course they are taught the theory but the practical application is so very different. In my first book I detail initial basic training and how such practical demonstrations at training school differ so radically to the real world of actual police work. On leaving the training schools with so many worthless paper qualifications they soon realize that they have absolutely no experience involving the management of many men, some with the lowly rank of detective constable with much more knowledge and accordingly harbouring resentment which in itself seriously affects morale. These are good able detectives, who have made a career choice not to study for a variety of reasons usually hinging on the fact that they could be on the piss seeking their next little naked victim, or meeting informants and then going on the lash probably with the proceeds of an insurance reward. As with the very poor documentaries, the majority of murders are now just a police public relations exercise, stage-managed to hide the real enormity of their failure. Parents, relatives, and friends are paraded at televised press conferences, pleading with the culprits to give themselves up. I don't quite get that one – they generally have to be caught or at least that's what happened in my day.

Wooden television appearances by the so-called investigating officer and weeping relatives are followed by filmed coverage of masses of uniforms thrashing the living daylights out of the countryside, white latex overalls on police officers, carrying many plastic bags of potential forensic evidence away from the scene. As the story loses media interest, some insignificant young lookalike does the last walk of the victim. I can't remember when any of these scenarios resulted in an arrest, but they actually delay any real detection work whilst mountains of pointless leads provided by the local nutters flood in bringing the real investigation to a grinding halt. Then of course, if such information is regarded as important and worthy of investigation the entire procedure depends on the quality of the detective who is given the responsibility of vetting all possible leads. How many murderers have been missed with poor collation of vital evidence only to be arrested some additional murders 'down the road' when found to have been in the system already. They are often highlighted during the initial investigation, but never interviewed. There have never been so many undetected murders and so many others thrown out of court for lack of real evidence.

In addition, there have never been so many convicted murderers released from prison terms of varying lengths, as evidence is proved to be unsafe. In the case of the murder of TV presenter Jill Dando an obviously innocent weirdo, Barry George, who was unable to defend himself effectively, was convicted and forgotten. He had a history of strange incidents, all sexually motivated and so tenuous was the evidence available that George was freed eight years later by the Court of Appeal. The question must be asked whether the evidence was "made to fit?" He is now proved to be innocent, but the arresting officers have never been taken to account. If he was indeed innocent the questions must be asked regarding the fact that gunpowder residue was found on his clothing. Only recently has a witness come forward and been believed by the media, but ignored by the original investigation in relation to a good description of the actual perpetrator. A swarthy male of eastern European appearance was seen near the murder scene of the BBC Crimewatch presenter's house. Despite his release from prison as a result of evidence unreliability Mr George continues to be denied compensation.

The conviction of Sion Jenkins for the murder of his step daughter, Billy Jo Jenkins has been declared unsafe, as it relied only on the forensic evidence of her blood on his clothes. Whilst never stated openly, the Appeal Judges must have considered the fact that the presence of the blood spots was much too convenient in the absence of other evidence. I had, in a detailed letter, informed the Jenkins' defence team that evidence such as this is commonly fabricated by investigating officers in the absence of real evidence. My assistance was acknowledged, but I was never called as a witness. Despite these publicized criminal acts of perjury and total corruption of the evidence, the so-called investigating officers are generally never brought to justice. No wonder similar acts are regularly perpetrated in the knowledge that the full force of the law will never fall on them and if it should they will inevitably be protected from any serious criminal charges as happened with such sad consequences for Stefan Kiszko.

The murder of Lesley Molseed is such a typical example of corruption of evidence and procedures on so many levels that it is certainly worthy of a detailed explanation. Lesley Susan Molseed was 11-years-old when she was murdered on the 5th October 1975. This is the same era as so many other corrupt incidents such as Jimmy Savile, the miners' strike and the paedophile Cyril Smith MP, who was well-known for his sexual activities involving children in the Rochdale area. He was protected by the same force where the murdered child lived and which assisted with this murder investigation. Stefan Ivan Kiszko, a 23-year-old tax clerk, was wrongly convicted of her sexual assault and murder. He served 16 years in prison after being wrongly convicted of these offences in what was described as 'the worst miscarriage of justice of all time' by one outraged Member of Parliament. Kiszko was released from prison in 1992 after further examination of forensic evidence showed that he could not have committed the crime. Kiszko died one year later and Ronald Castree was eventually found guilty of the crimes on November 12th 2007.

The little girl's body was found in a remote layby with 12 stab wounds. Her clothing had not been disturbed but the body had been laid in a 'pose' and the killer had ejaculated over her underwear. At the time of the hunt four teenage girls claimed Kiszko had indecently exposed himself to them and had repeated the act a month after the murder to one of the girls on Bonfire Night. Of course this was all the evidence required to suspect Kiszko of the murder and at the time the police concentrated on prosecuting him whilst ignoring other leads. Without doubt Kiszko had an idiosyncratic lifestyle which included a negligible social life and an odd habit of recording car registration numbers of drivers who annoyed him. There is no doubt he suffered learning difficulties.

He was arrested on the 21st December 1975 and the police 'found' a bag of sweets and girlie magazines in his car. He was subjected to three days of intensive questioning after which he admitted to the offence, because in his disturbed mind he would then be released and allowed to go home whilst the investigation continued and he would be proved innocent. This belief in itself demonstrates his simple thinking abilities and clearly the police took advantage of this. He was the only suspect as all other 'leads' were discounted despite strong evidence to the contrary. After all he had confessed which certainly did not assist his cause. Kiszko was not automatically entitled to a solicitor as is the case today and indeed it was not until the Police And Criminal Evidence Act of 1984 that such a requirement became law. Kiszko was never asked if he wanted a solicitor and was never cautioned until well after the police had decided he was the only suspect. He was charged with the murder on Christmas Eve 1975 and his trial commenced on 7th July 1976. Kiszko was defended by David Waddington QC, who was later to become the Home Secretary, and prosecuted by Peter Taylor QC, who later became the Lord Chief Justice and the author of the infamous Hillsborough Report.

Of course, back then the majority of the jury believed the police evidence, however flawed it proved to be. Kiszko stated his admission was purely to pacify the police who were then 'nice' to him on his admission. The conduct of his defence left much to be desired, but even his solicitor believed him to be guilty. He was found guilty after five hours and 35 minutes deliberation, but only on a 10 out of 12 majority verdict. The learned judge commended all the witnesses particularly Detective Sergeant John Ackroyd and Detective Superintendent Dick Holland. Kiszko was eventually sent to Wakefield prison where he was kept apart from other prisoners on what is known as Rule 43 for his own safety. Despite this he was attacked several times and throughout his sentence his mental health deteriorated as he was moved from prison to prison and into several mental health establishments.

For eight years Kiszko's mother campaigned for his case to be reopened. He would never admit to the offence and as a consequence would never be considered for parole. His mother contacted JUSTICE the Human Rights organization and they eventually had the case reopened. The case was referred back to West Yorkshire Police where Detective Superintendent Trevor Wilkinson conducted the investigation and immediately found several glaring errors. Witnesses were found to confirm Kiszko's alibi of visiting a grave in Halifax and visiting a nearby shop. These witnesses had never been properly interviewed by the investigating officers and whatever evidence they gave totally contradicted the decision to prosecute Kiszko and therefore show the murder as detected. The witnesses were not called by his defence team who may not even have been aware of their existence as of course their use would have resulted in a not guilty verdict.

At the time of the reopened investigation it was also established that Kiszko had a physical problem which prevented him producing sperm, so consequently could not have ejaculated over the victim. This fact was known to the investigating officers. The four young girls all admitted lying 'for a laugh.' Whilst all the detail is significant it is sufficient to say that Kiszko was by the time of his release mentally ill. He was awarded a derisory £500,000 most of which he did not receive due to his death a year after his release.

The point to all the above detail is of course what actually happened to the once commended police officer who by the time of his release had been denounced by the trial judge, the Molseed family and the local media. Detective Superintendent Holland and Ronald Outteridge, the forensic scientist, were formally charged with 'doing acts tending to pervert the course of justice' by allegedly suppressing evidence, namely the results of the semen tests from Kiszko and from the victim's body. The defence counsel at an early pre-trial hearing before magistrates, proved that a fair trial was impossible for Holland. He was guilty, deliberately so and should have appeared in court to answer the charges, but it was once again brushed away.

Holland came to public prominence in yet another flawed investigation into the Yorkshire Ripper and M62 'bomber' Judith Ward, who had her conviction ruled as unsafe in 1992. Having once had these investigations regarded as his finest hours in 35 years of police service Holland was subsequently demoted, four years after Kiszko's conviction. As I have said, Holland's defence barrister had argued that his conviction would be unsafe due to the passage of time and would make a fair trial impossible. In yet another example of the naivety of magistrates they agreed and the matter was not sent for trial. Holland died in 2007 at the age of 74 and remains yet another example of the corrupt practices of the West Yorkshire Police and their ability to avoid legal retribution despite the weight of evidence.

The trial judge and West Yorkshire Police have apologized for this dreadful miscarriage of justice, but surely such a miscarriage has been further exacerbated with the lack of prosecutions against the men who deliberately fabricated evidence to ensure a conviction of an innocent man. Kiszko for so many years suffered amazing hardships in prison, which eventually caused his mental illness and death on release. So long after these events David Cameron is proclaiming the police to be 'relatively honest,' but the corruption and fabrication remains.

In yet another but simpler example of the one law for us and one for them traffic constable John Wetherall, 34, was dismissed from the South Yorkshire Force in what must certainly be a first and a sign of the times. This man had 10 years unblemished service in the force, and was career-minded, looking to be promoted at any opportunity. His life is now in ruins. Clearly the offence must have been serious, much more than a Deputy Chief Constable in Manchester prosecuted for driving at 120mph on the M6 toll road. He received a token sentence which did not involve the automatic ban that the rest of the speeding public suffers for the same offence. Wetherall actually drove his car over the force boundary into Nottinghamshire which is hardly crossing into Russia, and kissed a woman who got into his car. There was no sex or even attempts at sex. Being a traffic car, the interior and exterior is constantly filmed by two separate cameras. PC Wetherall, being aware of this, removed the videos of his married lady friend's activity in the police car and put them in his locker. The grave differences in police practices of today and my day, now become apparent. A fellow PC entered his secured locker claiming to be seeking a video for evidence, found the offending videos and handed them to the supervisory officers, who, on PC Wetherall's return from holiday, took disciplinary action against him, resulting in dismissal. Obviously, he was astounded at the dual standards in the force. Because in the same week a high ranking officer in the same force was caught having sex with a blonde female inspector with no serious disciplinary consequences. Again in the same force, continuing to perpetuate the double standards and be in no doubt that every force is the same; a sergeant was caught having sex with a married woman in a police car.

Not so sexually different from the heady days of my uniformed service at Bootle Street, Manchester. Everybody from the Superintendent down had secret liaisons both on and off duty. Officers had the comfort of their own offices whilst us lower sprogs had to make do with any position available. On nights, there were more police cars on deserted car parks, rocking from side to side than there were patrolling the streets. Most officers had a favourite female on every beat. Some of the less choosy had the same one and a change was as good as a rest as far as the 'lady' was concerned. If a beat boundary had to be crossed to achieve "the end" so to speak, then it was. Whatever the circumstances the job got done, in a fashion, the figures showed some effort, arrests more by accident than deliberate police work and everyone was happy.

Prince Charles, in recognition of the total failure of the police at the highest levels of security, announced in the Daily Mail that Royal Security is now in the hands of the army in the form of an ex-special forces officer. The Royal Protection Department and its Old Etonian head, Commander Peter (Lord) Loughborough, who is responsible for day to day security, has had to accept this embarrassment. It has, at last been recognized by the faceless powers that be, that security is no longer a game. It is no longer a promotion exercise, but a department where experience rather than examination results is the vital ingredient. When one compares the service records of the two, there really is no contest.

The history books and accounts up to the present day are littered with similar examples of fabricated evidence. With regular monotony tragic individuals are released from lengthy prison sentences amid a blaze of publicity having had evidence re-examined, DNA checked again with modern methods and the like. The culture existing in the police during my early days ran amok in the knowledge that there was no one to effectively criticize their conduct and any corruption of flimsy evidence was fair game to ensure a conviction. Should the police of today continue in this manner with selected cases, involving so much public sympathy then people would be falling in behind their police again, they would believe they were being protected and give their support accordingly. The old adage of 'your turn' comes to mind. Unfortunately the police generally do not know where to 'draw the line' and attack all and sundry with corrupted evidence, so badly prepared that this conduct is being recognized and prevented, wherever possible but still no prosecutions of police are taking place as a result of such actions, except on very, very, rare occasions.

Such evidential fabrication is what Manchester 'legal eagle' Mark O'Connor relies upon. His ability to swoop and dissect a police prosecution file is legendary among Manchester's accused population. He successfully identifies the breaks in evidence continuity, the abuses of process, the downright fabrications and police lies that are all his bread and butter. His successful acquittals of those initially facing an apparent wealth of irrefutable evidence, is as I have already mentioned legendary. There is little doubt that his address book of learned counsel is second to none, all wishing to represent his clients in the knowledge that the initial investigation has left no stone unturned and a successful end result is considerably enhanced by Mark's initial preparation and detailed instructions.

As flagged up earlier you have to ask yourself; is Manchester Special Branch so poorly staffed with men, so devoid of initiative and forward planning that they couldn't take a "little bit" of evidence with them, just in case?

His Royal 'well protected' highness

Forget the Royal baby of 2013. Back in the day decades before, I was regarded as a police marksman. A title earned as I have already related by hitting the target, not far away with about six rounds out of the 10 supplied. With such skills I was attached for the night to the 'James Bonds' of the City, the Special Branch and placed on VIP bodyguard duty.

The current Royal baby's great-grandfather Prince Phillip needed guarding in the 1970s. And strangely, yet totally in keeping with police logic, I formed part of the assignment of super-tuned 'bodyguards', but, of course, without the gun despite now being fully certificated and raring to shoot anybody.

Because of their collective darkness phobia and the 'we don't do nights' attitude, which appeared to exist in the Special Branch at all ranking levels, I was placed on night duty to assist in the protection of Prince Phillip. I was assigned with other officers from the Drug Squad and a couple of real bodyguards from New Scotland Yard. One of the regular Manchester SB officers, who had lost the office raffle, also joined us to act as liaison with the regular Scotland Yard Royal Protection contingent. In the halcyon days of no real security issues there were only about six of us for this duty. However we were all finely honed into this small unit of highly-trained manpower, braced for any eventuality and waiting to spring into action at a second's notice, but of course armed only with our equally highly trained hands as we were not allowed the guns with which we had been drilled. On this occasion when we were assigned to guard His Royal Highness, Prince Philip was on a visit to Salford University as Honorary Vice Chancellor. Although, it must be said, that among us HRH was better known as Phil the Greek as Ken Chaplin, of the A Division, was a stoker on his last ship.

This was an annual visit and great play was made of the fact he would be treated as 'just one of the boys,' because he was to sleep in an ordinary student room on a normal landing with all the people as normal and ordinary as you find in any university. But one must remember that the word 'normal' is hardly ever used for the long-haired, drinking, cannabis-smoking marauders who populated this building, usually sleeping something off or shagging until the one class of the day later in the afternoon. The dormitory building was three storeys high with small single en-suite rooms. They were all clean but sparsely furnished with only a single bed, a wardrobe and a bedside table. Nobody publicized the fact that the entire floor was cleared of students and HRH had his own entrance to the building in case he bumped into one of the 'unclean' long-haired greasy reprobates. The rooms in question and indeed the landing corridor had been newly decorated and kept empty to rid them of the smell of paint and the lingering aromas of the unwashed masses of regular occupants for a couple of weeks. All the rooms had been newly furnished and yet the whole set up must have appeared to be a Vietnamese mud hut to Phil who was used to a little better even on board his destroyer.

Phil had the room farthest from the entrance staircase so in the event of an assassination attempt we would fall on our swords in protecting His Royal Highness. The room next door was occupied by his Royal Protection armed Scotland Yard bodyguard. Next to this was his valet John, clearly adept at trapping a bus ticket between the cheeks of his bottom an art ably displayed as he minced from room to room looking busy, prim and proper, but in reality doing nothing at all except to show off his tight little arse just in case one of us was to jump out of the closet. John had brought his own furniture in the shape of his trusty ironing board. There was then a gap of four locked rooms to act as a barrier from any noise for the sleeping Prince in case he woke up as a frog as in all good nursery stories. At the entrance end to the corridor was then a room, cleared of furniture, newly decorated and prepared as a buffet with every type of alcoholic drink and sandwich, small snacks, even biscuits and Horlicks – the latter apparently His Royal Highnesses' favourite night time tipple. The bodyguard contingent also occupied the room next door which again had been cleared and replaced with a few uncomfortable chairs for our use, probably deliberately uncomfortable as of course we were supposed to be warily patrolling the darkened corridors and outside perimeter in our capacity as unarmed minders.

Our duty was to initially arrive early and search all the rooms from where the students had been made homeless some weeks before, taking all their pin-up photos from the walls, books and drug paraphernalia. Of course we had to search all rooms including His

Royal Highness' next best thing to a tent. It was clearly set out for the maximum of appearance, but it was still strange to see the official Palace released photo of Her Majesty the Queen, diamond tiara and all displayed on a bedside table. I think from recent events they have amply displayed the fact that they are however a very close couple and they both gain strength from each other and so a little photo may have got Phil through the night. On the other bedside table was a wooden box about nine inches by nine inches containing every proprietary medicine you could want for the prevention and cure of a cold, sore throat, reluctant bowels and all other minor ailments which could easily inflict upon him in deepest Salford.

John, the valet, continued to mince about, fluttering his eyelids with a wiggle of his tight black pants. All of us in the temporary James Bond contingent had skated a bit close to the transvestite wind, usually by a drunken mistake in some darkened club, but none of us felt any urge towards John other than perhaps to give him a swift kick. Whilst immaculately attired in full valet livery I thought he would probably have been happier in a maid's outfit, which would have been much more in keeping with all his other effeminate traits.

The Prince's accommodation was on the top floor of this three storey building. The floors below were occupied by students, females, specially selected, with strict instructions for silence and no unruly behaviour. The fact that bombs, tend to explode in an upwards direction, especially in flimsy modern buildings had not occurred to anyone. No one searched the other floors, there were no SAS snipers, no dogs, or mine detectors as today and in reality the entire security issue was a virtually unarmed, unprotected joke.

However, Manchester's finest were on hand and braced for any eventuality. During the early evening HRH was at a civic reception in the Town Hall and at the arranged time in what was a very detailed calculated timetable the Prince was to arrive at the reception doors to the student accommodation. At this time he had a bit of an entourage from the university who had also been at the Town Hall reception. We were braced at the entrance, hands crossed at waist height, as in the movies, looking unsmiling at the assembled crowd and would have worn sunglasses in typical FBI fashion had it not been so dark.

We joined forces with the existing team and escorted HRH into the building and up the stairs toward his accommodation. To the right took him to his corridor and room at the end. The carefully planned timetable allowed for 15 minutes in the students bar, a fact we had not been privy to and which caused some confusion as we attempted to change his direction whilst being corrected by the men from the Yard. Turning to the left chose the route past the students bar, where despite the rigid timetable Phil, feigned surprise at 'bumping' into the bar where his 'surprise' was equalled by the surprised masses of students, chosen to occupy the bar. For such a well and acutely trained protection detail such a detour, planned or not was the makings of a nightmare, especially in the company of a crowd of glorified schoolchildren all vying for attention through childish remarks and actions, which could even have been an attempted Rag Day kidnap stunt.

Into the bar walked the genial HRH still feigning surprise as he marches right into the middle of them, shook a few hands and rested on the bar. He declined a pint, or anything else for that matter, was called "mate" by the resident 'cheekie chappie' before he was dragged off to Salford University's equivalent of the Tower of London.

Genuinely pleased and somewhat pissed cheering students jostled for position to HRH's ever so polite amusement. His 15 minutes duty completed, HRH bade goodnight saying: "Fucking off to bed now! Good night." This, of course, to those who have had the undoubted pleasure of his company will recognize it as his normal vocabulary, a stronghold from his Royal Navy days. Of course, the students loved it. The effing HRH brought the house down.

As he tottered along the corridor clearly suffering the effects of the civic reception, HRH never even looked in at the buffet and retired to his room dutifully followed by mincing John now happy that his boss had returned. He had been known to reappear some minutes later, 'just to keep the chaps on their toes' so we were all on guard. His valet, who had minced after him into his room, reappeared after assisting him into his 'jim jams' as he so fondly called them.

Then we had the night to get through, and all the food and drink left for our use. The Royal Standard was flying on the roof as it did whenever members of the Royal family were in residence and was supposed to remain so for as long as they stayed. Being an obvious target for souvenir-hunting students, it was removed to be replaced in the morning for the 10 minute exit.

Obviously, with HRH in residence and all the possible dangers associated with such an important guest, all security factors were mentioned at length at a briefing, but casually ignored by alleged experienced and expert security operatives in relation to a full and detailed bomb search. With equal concern and being trained to such a finely-tuned state we all wandered into the buffet room. We were bodyguards and of course the food had to be tasted and checked for poisons in case an assassin had tried a different method and in case HRH got up for a midnight snack. John, the valet, joined us, minced into the room, loved the masculine, hairy-arsed company as we told him a few jokes, some mildly homophobic, but harmless and by 6.30am he was as pissed as we were.

Clearly and totally out of character he had not hot showered, shaved and changed his lovely pressed outfit. His pert little effeminate face drained of colour as he heard the boss' bedroom door open. To make matters worse, HRH appeared at his door. Down the corridor, he bellowed: "John, where's my fucking shirt?" The door slammed shut. John, close to fainting, scurried along the corridor: "Coming, Sir." And in a flash he appeared with the shirt from his room, luckily ironed the evening before having then spent a night on the tiles with Manchester's finest.

The exit from the building went as planned. We waved goodbye to Phil the Greek and off we went to Greek Chris' in Piccadilly for breakfast. This was a café which opened for 24 hours and for most of which Chris was in the premises. He wore more grease in his clothes and his thinning hair, than was used in the frying pan. Being of the same nationality we gave Chris Phil's regards. Chris was very impressed. He never dreamed that we actually did police work and, especially something as outrageous as guarding the 'King.' In the past he had only experienced our drunken visits at 4am to consume his free bacon butties believing that we were on the way home after a night's shagging.

ONE OF THE BUOYS AND ANOTHER BIT OF BODYGUARDING

Ted Heath was preaching: "Buy British!" He was Prime Minister and was bravely visiting the Northern territories when he stayed at the Piccadilly Hotel, in the centre of Manchester. It was then the four star accommodation it claimed to be and not the tired disgrace it deteriorated into accommodating only air crew until being refurbished and bought by another hotel chain.

An entire floor was taken to accommodate Mr Heath and a couple of his flunkies. The general security of the floor and all the rooms was again checked by Manchester's Finest. I was again in attendance in my capacity of unarmed police marksman and general bar and buffet taster. Whilst dealing with the security aspects of Mr Heath's room we checked his wardrobe, more in the vain hope of finding a porn book of schoolboys rather than a bomb. We had no grounds for such a wish, other than the regular suggestions of perhaps a level of homosexuality. All his suits were immaculate and clearly labelled with the signature of his Singapore tailor. None were made in England.

Ted Heath had all the same catering services as HRH at Salford University. The attractive buffet and bar dutifully prepared by the hotel chef was not even examined, or appreciated and certainly not used on his return.

Where Prince Phillip at least pretended to be one of the boys, Ted returned to the hotel, pompous and above it all, taking our presence for granted with a look of disdain as he glanced at our disheveled Marks & Spencer's best, draped over an armchair in readiness for diving into the buffet. Toffee-nosed Ted retired without even a polite goodnight.

There has always been gossip about lifelong bachelor Ted's sexuality and if he wasn't, he does a good impression. We were all disappointed he didn't have a rent boy smuggled in purely to satisfy all the empty rumours which abounded at the time. He was like so many Tory Prime Ministers close to Sir Jimmy Savile, who at that point might well have been the predatory paedophile he proved to be, but catching him was not an option as we all had too much drinking and shagging to do of our own. Looking back it should have been more of a priority – but we were policing in the fashion of the day. There were in fact many police officers much closer to Savile in both Manchester and Yorkshire, where he preyed on youngsters both male and female. They closely socialized with him and he even boasted that they actively protected him against many complaints of his sexual assaults. Now that his activities are so widely known, as are those of Cyril Smith MP, it really does beg the obvious questions of whether several officers actually indulged in the same practices whilst in his social circle.

Back at the Piccadilly Hotel we had on that wonderful night with Prime Minister Ted another celebrity guest very much on our radar. Dave Allen, the Irish comedian, now deceased having died in 2005 aged 68 – strangely enough the same year Ted shuffled off this mortal coil. Dave Allen launched his satire against the absurdities of life and of religion – God Bless him he turned up on that night at the Piccadilly to give us some happy memories. He regularly attacked the Roman Catholic Church having been educated by the Catholic Christian Brothers, who were notorious for beatings of pupils. Such behavior by these priests turned Dave into an atheist and one must wonder how much he really knew of their sadistic and homosexual activities, whether he was subjected to this and how his act would have changed as more and more Catholic priests were 'outed.' He was starring at the Golden Garter, a theatre club situated in Wythenshawe, which is South of Manchester. To appreciate the strange decision to locate such a centre of entertainment in such an area of wanton criminality as Wythenshawe requires an explanation. It was the largest council estate in Europe at that time. It was also an area of petty theft, incest and many so called cot deaths, which based on today's techniques some could have been murders, but unfortunately there wasn't the forensic means through detailed analysis, to detect this type of offence.

Being at its peak during this time, the Piccadilly Hotel was the best Manchester had to offer and on this particular night it was full except for the wasted rooms on Ted Heath's floor. Dave Allen was regarded as a big star during these times. I didn't personally find him funny that is until I spent a night with him, or rather in his company. He had his own popular TV programme and even got laughs from having a piece of finger missing. However, he had a smooth, confident style and I suppose he was very likeable. The Prime Minister must have been amused by him as he was allowed to stay on

Ted's floor as the hotel had blundered by not keeping his reserved room.

The Prime Minister was in bed by 1am having ignored his buffet. His Scotland Yard entourage gave a few drunken weak instructions to our increasingly drunken bodyguard contingent, which in reality only appeared to highlight the dreadful inadequacies of Royal Protection even in those days. They gave no consideration to a variety of potential security breaches and, once they had retired to their room, we were manning the corridor without a gun between us. Clearly nothing has improved. Recently Prince Charles showed his distrust of police protection and tried to use the Army and during the same period Princess Anne detained a nutter in her house that had passed all semblance of uniformed security for an apparent job interview.

Ted had gone to bed, wet dreams about sailing surely on his mind and weighing anchor off the coast of Jersey and all the joys that the Channel Islands held for sailors like him. Now having had our security briefing, we were duly tucking into the smoked salmon and chicken legs when Dave Allen arrived. He liked a drink. He was hungry and all the London protection stiffs had gone to bed, being tired of trailing around Manchester fighting off demonstrators from the same student ranks, which had just a few weeks earlier welcomed HRH.

Dave Allen joined us and to say he enjoyed a drink proved to be an understatement. He stayed with us for ages and must have gone through his entire act. In return, he suffered our jokes, jokes he politely agreed he should be using, but without the slurred speech. He knew Ted Heath was in the building and cracked the gag: "Ted Heath was sailing in the Solent and fell overboard.

He was floating in his life jacket when one of his lackies asked: 'Shall I throw you a buoy Sir?"

"What?" Ted replied, "Not now this is an emergency!"

Another funny story which remains with me from that night went like this: "I was just walking through the hotel reception when a newly married couple came to the desk. The husband was worse for wear and somewhat tired and emotional. The bride said: "We have just got married. Can we have our room?" The receptionist asked: "Do you have any reservations?" The young bride answered: "Yes, I don't take it up the arse."

Isn't it funny, you can be enthralled by a comedian and laugh non-stop, but can't remember a single joke the next day and for that matter most of the months afterwards.

Not Predjudiced, Not Biased, Not Just Colour....But Commonsense

Such duties as bodyguarding Royalty and politicians were rare. We were constantly executing search warrants, in areas known for drug abuse and some of the dives we raided had to be seen to be believed. Whilst driving through Moss Side shortly after noon, having just left the magistrates courts on route back to the Didsbury area for lunchtime cocktails, a general radio message interrupted our social planning and it related to a man on a cycle, indecently exposing himself in Platt Lane Park. The vision of this episode attracted us to responding and indeed being a cyclist of some repute during my younger days I could not understand how he could maintain an erection on a cycle for so many differing reasons but mainly due to avoidance of disheveled clothing, bunched in the groin area.

Anyway, we drove into the park and there he was, dressed as described on the radio. We brought him to a stop with a blast of the siren from behind, which in itself could have given him a heart attack. As we got out of the car, he jumped off the cycle. Strangely he proved to be very well spoken and dressed immaculately. Had we stopped the correct person? He was wearing a white shirt and tie. His trousers were pressed and his shoes carefully polished. The outfit was coordinated with a smart gabardine trench coat, buttoned all the way up the front and tied at the waist with a casual knotted belt. It wasn't the norm to search 50-year-olds, but I had noticed bare flesh above his knee and moved the coat to gain a better view. This was prevented by our cyclist and so we opened the entire coat, only to collapse in fits of laughter. He was wearing a shirt and tie which were cut off at his upper chest and his immaculately pressed trousers finished just above the knees and were tied by cord. The remainder of his body was fully exposed and naked and explained in one act of revelation how he managed the erection whilst cycling.

On another occasion we raided a Pakistani-occupied council house coincidentally close to the same park. Whilst not being particularly prejudiced I can honestly say that I had no real time for any of them. They were not fit to be treated as equals, they were not used to it in their own country, so why should we bend over backwards with over the top PC. The house was filthy, smelt like a farmyard and even had a goat and two chickens in the front room, wallowing in their own excrement. Also living in the three bedroomed house were 10 adults, who appeared to sleep in shifts, in the same bed with the same unwashed bed clothes, and six children. There is no doubt that during this time such immigrants were treated as the second class citizens they clearly were, just by virtue of how they chose to live. Today of course, many still reside in the same conditions, but are considered equal in the eyes of the law and politicians. The judiciary and the politicians should have a crash course on the conditions the police, even today are forced to work in whilst remaining so PC. And alarmingly even today, officers can be suspended and even sacked for calling them a Paki. What is going on, when they don't behave as civilized in a Western society and then expect all the frills that go with it?

After leaving the police I employed Don Robertson, an ex-detective sergeant, who had suffered a 'there but for the grace of God' moment that ended up as a criminal charge for which he was found not guilty. I had discredited his main prosecution witness by simple, but difficult door to door enquiries in Liverpool. Whilst he escaped imprisonment with my endeavors and a not guilty verdict as a result, he had to resign from the police on what they said were disciplinary issues which usually meant: 'You lucky bastard, we know you are guilty.' So they got rid of him.

When he left the police he got a security job at Manchester International Airport with a firm which refurbished airplane interiors. Planes used on Pakistani routes from Manchester to Islamabad, were refurbished more often as some first-time travellers urinated and defecated where they sat, totally oblivious to the fact that the plane had toilets. Eventually the metal components, when treated to a quick dose of what Pakistani bowel movements had to offer rusted and rotted through the entire seating frame. I suspect that Hammerite could have patented Asian bowel movements as a rust remover.

Robertson being a lazy bastard in the police must have continued with his work ethic and was later made redundant and more out of pity rather than expertise, I employed him as manager in my sales department. Having effectively saved his life from the police prosecution and now given him employment I was sure I could have the expected loyalty and effort in return. He was provided with a credit card for general company expenses, which he chose to use to entertain his cronies still in the police with no benefit to the business whatsoever. He never acquired a new client. In my mind this was theft, he was just playing the big shot and we parted company. Amazing how friends thank you.

Whilst earlier in my career I was stationed at Didsbury Police Station, Detective Sergeant Ronnie Brookes, who was stationed at Longsight Police Station, dealing with a much lower standard of 'clientele' contracted Bell's Palsy after searching under a mattress in an Asian house. Is there any wonder prejudices exist in the police.

Flats occupied by the dropout English were also found to be in similar terrible conditions. The kitchens were filthy. Pots were piled everywhere, with the floors covered in rotting grub and takeaway food cartons. The furniture was inevitably falling apart and the bedrooms filthy. The bedding had not been washed for months and clothes littered the floor. Underwear, both male and female, often well skid-marked and filthy were littered everywhere. We used to see such places often, in varying locations, as we went about our Drug Squad duties and the occupants always appeared to be wearing the same clothes and for that matter I suppose the same underwear, which really does fuel the imagination. One of my venerable colleagues in the Drug Squad actually had a preference for women in soiled underwear and unwashed nether regions, but even he drew the line with some of these female individuals. I will spare his blushes in case he's cleaned up his act, so no naming and shaming in this chapter.

Asians with farm yards in their front rooms brings to mind another story which involved yet again a further use of straw for carpeting. Based on information, totally fictitious as it proved we executed a search warrant on a terraced house in Rusholme, now a hot bed for terrorist activities and madras curries again causing a 'hot bed' due to an involuntary follow through. There was a large new Rover parked outside. We knocked on the door which fell open and on sneaking in we could hear shouting from the cellar. It sounded like a fight. At the bottom of the stairs our quiet entry was brought to an abrupt halt as again the men at the front collapsed in fits of laughter and were pushed further into the room by the following horde that could not see the cause of the amusement. The cellar smelt like a stable with a back ground hint of cheap perfume and baby oil. The floor was carpeted with straw. A large spring was attached to a wooden beam and hanging from this a leather harness which supported a well trussed middle-aged man, bound in leather strapping, supporting his body weight, a riding bit in his mouth, whilst pulling on his nether regions giving a perfect erection which was in the mouth of 'his jockey.' He was happily bouncing from the spring whilst being whipped throughout the 'blow job.' The 'jockey' attired in full riding gear, but crotchless apparel proved to be a transvestite, blonde wig, pierced nipples and a riding helmet smelling of the cheap perfume and the baby oil amply sprayed to prevent chafing amidst mid-bounce.

What a sight but what do we do? This was hardly criminal and certainly had some immediate appeal, but under differing gender circumstances and perhaps without the straw. John Schumsky who I can now name, a late friend, could not resist taking the reins and giving a giddy up to the 'horse', up the stairs and onto the street. We found his keys amongst his clothing which we threw into the car and set him on his way, still clad in his fetching leather outfit driving his luxury Rover in a fashion which coincidentally resembled the use of 'Rocking Horse' petrol. This was actually a driving style favoured by female drivers with manual gearsticks and poor clutch control.

By an amazing coincidence, whilst in the Drug Squad, we executed a search warrant on yet another terraced house in Moss Side. It proved to be occupied by people connected to those, who had allegedly planted a bomb in a dustbin. The same bomb which I had carried innocently in the bin, in the rear of a police van full of fighting Irish navvies. This had been found outside the Italian Consulate when I was the uniformed van driver at Bootle Street Police Station during my early days.

We arrested them for possession of drugs. As was the practice we carried bits of cannabis in case we found nothing, which was the case here and as a result they decided to take the piss feeling that they were totally vindicated and proved to be innocent. It was an established culture that individuals such as these had to recognize the pecking order and we had to be seen as a force to be feared. We were 'The Biggest Gang' and had to be seen to be so. However, such additional evidences proved to be unnecessary as they already had traces of cannabis in smoked cigarette ends and also traces of heroin on a blackened and burnt spoon. This was certainly a sign of the times and the increasing use of hard drugs. They would put crystals of the drug in a spoon which they would heat up with a lighter. The crystals would melt into a liquid which they would inject into their arms. When the veins in their arms totally collapsed from regular use due to the heavy addiction they used veins in the hands until they also collapsed. If they were still alive by the time all the obvious veins had collapsed they used the veins in their feet which inevitably affected their walking abilities.

This find was the first and only time I had ever come across real Class A drugs during my early Drug Squad days. Cocaine was also unheard of and whilst with my present knowledge, I am sure it existed, we just never came across it, but it became much more popular as I moved into the CID in Didsbury.

During my uniformed service I would see a white VW Beetle in the city, being driven by Kenny Pilkington who was said to be a drug dealer even in those early days at the tender age of 17. He was often arrested and as the years went by moved into cocaine dealing. I was told once by a dealer that the dealer never takes his own 'product.' Kenny didn't follow that philosophy and eventually his nasal passages collapsed as did more of his skull resulting in his death. One less dealer on the streets selling the stuff, but they get replaced by others unfortunately.

In searching the Moss Side house we found many posters and we quickly realized this was the same group who had planted the bomb and we immediately sought revenge as we awaited the arrival of the Special Branch to examine the politically-sensitive find. This terraced house had a typically small rear kitchen leading to the outside toilet. On the stove was a large cauldron of stew which smelt vile. It was vegetarian in keeping with their protesting hippy lifestyle. Of course being a vegetarian ensured they were 'healthy' and never lived off killed animals. This was rich for a gang of shitheads, who would have killed people with the bomb and were killing themselves with wanton drug use.

Somebody believed the stew could be improved by adding Pochin a lethal strong spirit distilled from potatoes and emptied about a gallon of it into the bubbling stew. The Pochin had been found under the stairs and clearly had been purchased from our friendly off-licence, which had been raided with the customs and excise only a couple of weeks before. From experience, it wasn't tested for taste. The fumes it gave off when raiding the manufacturing plant had initially burnt our nasal passages and backs of our throats rendering us dizzy and speechless. Of course this was a state we regularly experienced, but usually voluntarily on Carlsberg Special Brew and rum over an evening and not in the 30 seconds involved with this tasting session. Being daytime, the Special Branch took all the male occupants away leaving three smashed females to complete the evening meal of stew and stew with an innovative side dish of stew. However the stew was now bubbling away from the increased heat which was added with the flick of a dial on the oven, by one of the searching team and unnoticed by the abusive 'chefs' in their drug fuelled haze. That was until the bubbling Pochin fumes proved to be flammable as they met with the gas ring and blew the back windows out of the shanty-type kitchen extension.

There is little point detailing other such raids. They were all pretty much the same and rarely had the same comedy element related above. The usual working practice was to knock on the door, give them only seconds to answer before breaking it down and entering. Drugs were easily flushed down the toilet and we had to be quick to prevent this. On one occasion, John Schumsky, a 20 stone wrestling champion and 5th Dan in judo, knocked on a door. It wasn't opened in the allotted 10 seconds and Schumsky put his ample shoulder to the door, in a run from a few yards. This illustration of an unstoppable force hitting an immovable object had the desired effect. The lock gave the impression of exploding as did the hinges. The whole door came off and fell into the house. We ran in and couldn't find the home owner. We eventually did. He was unconscious under the front door, having almost opened it, before being trampled to unconsciousness by a score of Manchester's Finest.

SEARCHING .... MORE OF A PARTY THAN A DUTY

Friday nights were like all Friday nights everywhere in the world, except perhaps Muslim countries where Friday is Sunday, so to speak. We all met in the office at about 6pm waiting with anticipation, the forthcoming night on the piss. Before we left our city centre office and headed South we often had a bite to eat at a nearby restaurant which was regularly targeted by detectives from various departments. This particular establishment was well known to employ illegal immigrants and to continue with this employment structure the owner was happy to pay what he saw as an instant fine for his doubtful staff. In addition to his employment indiscretions the owner also operated an illegal casino on the first floor. He had a roulette wheel and a large card table for the regular poker school. Inevitably a couple of lower-end prostitutes also frequented the casino and entertained the Asian clientele in rooms on the third floor. Prostitutes were always fair game but the line was drawn at following Asians with a wet one.

In my early CID days I had a detective sergeant whom I drove on evening crime patrols. We visited this particular restaurant from the rear door, late into the evening and out of sight of the dining clientele. The owner was not in the kitchen and there were several new faces beavering away in the equatorial conditions. One of the regular staff mumbled something in the native tongue at which they all laughed. Under normal circumstances we would have had to accept that this conversation was likely to be piss-taking but what could we do? However my senior colleague had been a member of the magic circle since school days and before the force had decided to drop out of university and travel to India. He chose to be a travelling 'wizard' and walked from village to village performing his tricks for the simple and uneducated villagers in return for food and accommodation. In these fascinating travels he learnt Urdu which was a variation of many Indian and Pakistani dialects. It was understood by many without being a pure language or dialect – I suppose it's almost similar to Geordie and even Scouse in the UK. He returned to the UK having become proficient in this language and joined the police. In today's policing he would have been given his own department to placate the victimized minorities and arrange benefits and animal foodstuffs for the front room 'ornaments.' To say he was not amused at the mickey-taking by the kitchen staff was an understatement. In hysterical Urdu he ranted at all the staff and in no time had them lined up for a passport inspection. They were of course illegal and in some panic.

The owner burst into the kitchen. We of course knew him and yet the Sarge screamed at him in Urdu, being totally consumed by the disciplinary moment. He was so shocked that he replied in his own native tongue. Had the floor not been ankle deep in filth, chickens entrails and grease he would have thrown himself to his knees and kissed feet. Diplomacy came to the fore and the

Sarge allowed the boss to let his terrified 'illegal' staff return the following day with their documents.

We all knew this would never happen but it was an acceptable compromise under the circumstances. In keeping with the introduction of the newly established discipline we visited the upstairs casino and ignored the banquet on offer in the restaurant for the time being. The poker school was in full swing with a variety of players of several ethnic origins, Greeks, British, Italians and particularly a couple of Asians. The honesty stakes were well tested in this game where they were all very sharp and capable of cheating at any opportunity. Our presence unnerved a couple of the players and very soon there remained only the two Asians and a couple of Greeks. Sarge detected the Asians whispering in their home tongue and pretending to be discussing the catering and on standing closer could understand them with his grasp of Urdu. Of course, they were discussing their hands and cheating. Sarge sat in with a kitty provided by the panicking restaurant owner, who was by this stage merely glad to remain in business however tenuous in the light of the funds necessary for Sarge's stake. The game proceeded, the Asians discussed their hands and played accordingly only to have the Sarge drop out when they had a good hand and gamble when they were bluffing. The winnings were very impressive, we kept the initial stake as well as the instant fine for the earlier insults and of course enjoyed the resulting meal. We returned the following evening to find the owner and one other legal working feverishly in the absence of the rest of the illegal staff. The final punishment, well not actually, because we were of course hungry again but gave the poker a miss.

For entertainment we usually went up to Didsbury in South Manchester, an upper class area with large properties, many of which were divided into flats, occupied by female students from the teacher training college nearby. This area was also populated with the usual drug-taking flotsam, who on Friday nights were ignored. There was never any real intention of making any arrests, unless someone was stupid enough to deal cannabis in front of us in a pub or on a street corner.

As the shift started it was too early to hit the nightspots. Some colleagues went for the curry whilst others had a game of cards in the office. This was the order of most Fridays and with most of the lads it entailed a joint. I didn't smoke, so I tried burning a piece on a needle, which I then inhaled though never really recognized any effect. The smokers had a joint and some of them even dropped speed to get them through the long night. Speed ranged from 5mg dexamphetamine sulphate, known as Purple Hearts, to 25mg in capsule form, known as Black Bombers. Speed was in the pharmaceutical market place as slimming aids and was in great demand by many on the nightclub scene in Manchester and Wigan.

Throughout the card game, the dog handler was training his hapless hound Benji. Paul Giles always had fur-lined gloves to prevent a Ronnie Brookes incident in his mind remaining sterile in his own version of a marigold glove moment. Whenever Benji was in the office Paul would turn a glove inside out and use it as a furry beige Sooty, peeping up over his arm. The dog nodding away as he talked to it. Despite the fact he found it difficult to play cards with the glove inside out on his hand, he persevered and whenever Benji was around Paul had his fascinating little puppet peeping over his arm. Benji was certainly less suited to drug detection as any dog I have ever seen and simply could not concentrate on his excuse for training. His handler was becoming increasingly agitated and looked for the reason. Paul just ducked his gloved hand out of sight and the endless entertainment continued until Benji decided to have a nap, which was as often as his other occupation of begging for sandwiches, Kentucky Fried Chicken, or any other unhealthy snack provided by the lads who did not have an understanding wife who would cook at all hours. It all passed for entertainment as did Bill Kerr, an admirably straight member of this police flotsam, keen as ever, as he often dragged in an early prisoner he had been saving until he had time. He would put his head around the door, test the air quality and then had to adjourn to the sergeant's office, to prevent the prisoner smelling our smokes. Of course, we all offered to help with the physical confessionals and legendary detective 'Hoagy' Carmichael rolled his towel in readiness, but Bill usually had the situation sorted with his legal interview techniques, a quality many in the Drug Squad failed to grasp.

Search warrants were a common occurrence, often based on information from varied 'snouts' (paid informants), but often merely based on a hunch which of course was not the reason related to the learned magistrate at the time of the warrant application. As we searched various premises ranging from one bedroomed flats, terraced houses through the spectrum to wealthy and expensive premises throughout the Manchester area. 'Gilesey,' wherever he was, constantly harassed Benji with the fur glove to keep him out of the way as we were rushing about the flat turning over everything from beds, settees to dining tables, hollowed out books and so many other hiding places and in doing so were finding the odd parcel, hidden in some quite inspired hiding places. The freezer was thought to be inspired by the simple druggies and fish finger boxes were regarded as hiding places of real inspiration. What they didn't realize was the fact that they all used the same ideas, having boasted about them in a local pub in the company of a sprinkling of our informants.

The smaller packets in hollowed out books on the book shelf were numerous and clearly the users regarded us as phsycic. Of course, in many instances we were aided by our resident 'snouts' that also frequented the same pubs. We always claimed the dog was a waste of time and expense, as we always found the drugs first. This was hardly a surprise after all with Benji seeking Sooty on Giles' hand rather than a stash. It may also have had something to do with the fact that the officer in charge of the search warrant brought in the 'stash' to find in the absence of any real ingredients, especially if the users were regarded as local villains and not worthy of the 'office pardon.'

In many cases the flat occupants proved to be regular people, students seeking a career in law, or medicine, and unworthy of our fabricated finds and the dreadful effects a possession of drugs conviction could have on their future careers. In such cases, we would substitute the genuine cannabis for formula before any serious and unjust action was taken. Formula was a mixture of cannabis seeds, any old dried leaves and a few stalks. Gullible students, moving to the big city university would fall for this regularly in Moss Side. In all my wayward experience, totally innocent individuals were never arrested and charged.

However, certain individuals were often charged with offences they had not committed when evidence proving an offence they had committed was not forthcoming. This was the good old style of Life On Mars with its own particular form of justice and which certainly 'kept the lid on' by preventing wholesale criminality with a fear of instant justice. It was all known as 'your turn' and accepted to a degree, but of course, never totally as a prison sentence could have been the end result. Professional criminals had the strange belief that they were innocent until proven guilty, but where proof was in short supply on too many occasions then it was 'their turn.'

As the Friday evenings in Didsbury passed on with uneventful regularity we would move on from the pubs of which there were many, onto clubs which were also plentiful. In addition to the Irish clubs actually closer to our working area we had the Golden Garter, the strangely situated cabaret club. As mentioned earlier it was in the centre of Wythenshawe, a place populated by a more than average criminal element which specialized in burglary, theft, shoplifting, bestiality and even incest. These scrotes had a difficult choice on Saturday nights; it was a sheep or their sister.

Throughout these halcyon days I saw all the popular acts of the day, such as 'The Comedians' from Granada TV's popular show, Frank Carson, Tommy Cooper and, of course, Ken Dodd who must have been real value for the members of the audience, who actually paid. Doddy's show was very funny and went on and on and on and even these days aged 83 – he's still treading the boards for hours on end. He's a class comedy act well worth catching – it would be 'criminal' to miss him. And after his infamous tax trial in which he was represented by my old barrister pal George Carman he kept the tax gags flowing. One of my favourites was when he told the audience – "self assessment I invented it." A Liverpool jury duly delivered a not guily verdict – arise Sir Kenneth of Knotty Ash I'd say.

Pop groups which were just sliding from the pinnacle of their success also did the rounds. The Hollies, The Searchers, Wayne Fontana and The Mindbenders were typical of talent on display. Having experienced the free cabaret and, often, a chicken in the basket, we moved on to Didsbury Lodge, a hotel with a good nightclub in the cellar. This was on the Didsbury section and on a Friday night was populated by the older end of the female social scene and the 'mature' married barmaids from the Royal Oak and I use the term lightly. This was a pub situated directly opposite Didsbury police station. Arthur, a landlord of the old school, employed a group of mature types and coincidentally served large chunks of often mature cheese at lunch times.

They were attractive and due to their advancing years were very grateful and a few of us had our regulars. Should we fail to score, which was as unlikely as snow in Zambia, or merely wanted pastures new, we would then go down to Moss Side, the notorious black area, populated in the main by Jamaicans. There were numerous clubs, some were licensed, but perhaps, not for the hours of trade they had and some were merely the cellar of a house with loud reggae and no license at all known as a shebeen.

An alternative to "the Moss" as it was known, was Cheetham Hill, where Banjo a jovial stocky black of African origin, had a wonderful establishment. It was the large Victorian semi where he lived. The cellar was a bar and dining area, and he sold cannabis to the users on that side of the city. He had a hinged peephole in his front door which was opened to examine the caller before they were allowed entry through his heavily fortified door. On one occasion, a shotgun was discharged at him through the hole as he peered through the cannabis haze into the dark, clearer outside. It was fortunate that he was hit in the head or he could have been killed.

Due to his ethnic pedigree he had a forehead which must have been an inch thick and of the same consistency as ebony. The shotgun must have been cut too short and certainly past its sell by date. The power it generated was, however sufficient to embed a considerable number of shotgun pellets in his forehead, which took an eternity to remove at the nearby Jewish Hospital.

His wife was white and taught me reggae dancing. This was a very stimulating experience, especially under the influence of Red Stripe beer and rum, which was all that Banjo illegally stocked. The thigh thrusting, crutch rubbing dance took some explaining to my wife at the next 'Policeman's Ball.'

This "arduous" police work wasn't all fun. There were the normal shifts to work. We did of course undertake some real police work, making arrests to avoid the attentions of the discipline department, occasionally acting on information that members of the Drug Squad were actively engaged in the wholesale supply of drugs.

The small group in which I was involved did not involve themselves with the serious drug dealing, but did spend a great deal of time observing individuals who were known to associate with various officers and in doing so catch them in the act of dealing and then watch the officer squirming as he tried to square the charge for his 'pal' whilst he himself was being threatened with exposure by the prisoner. Such activities took us late into the night and on into the early morning as the clubs and unlicensed shebeens had to have their regular visits. With such a vigorous life of law enforcement and social activity I would regularly arrive home at 4am from a 9am to 5pm day shift. However much fun this appeared to be it certainly took its toll.

Not all the staff came out of the Drug Squad unscathed. In later years, sometime after my service I learned of men being addicted to cocaine and to a lesser degree cannabis. Many marriages failed. Some wives couldn't cope with the long hours and the limp excuses for the smell of alcohol and prostitutes' perfumes, mingling with a ripe goat curry. Milkmen were also threatening legal action, having the living daylights frightened out of them when finding men asleep in their cars on the driveway of their homes rather than risk the wife's wrath or suffering from the changing of the door locks once again.

Ian Morton fared worse than the rest of us. His wife refused to cook for him if he wasn't home at usual office hours which was impossible under normal police circumstances and certainly so in the Drug Squad. He was constantly finding his food in the dog as opposed to the oven. He drank like a fish and, finally, became an alcoholic. In the latter stages of his problem he contracted

TB and left the police. I have only recently learned that he died some years after, having never really recovered from the arduous results of 12 months in the Drug Squad. For my part the eating and drinking into the early hours, removed the lining from my stomach, giving me ulcers and irritability which continues to today. Ian was one of a family of three, all policemen and sons of Bill Morton, by then retired from the police.

One of his brothers, Rod, made a success of a security business. The third, whose name I forget was moved on while working nights in the South Manchester area of Withington for what was regarded as strange behaviour, which I will not detail, but suffice to say did not involve sex or dishonesty. Certainly a greater degree of strange could be found among his psychopathic colleagues who were still busy raping, pillaging, burgling and thieving with the apparent approval of the hierarchy.

During my druggy days, I grew my hair long and sported a beard and in doing so could remain relatively unnoticed in a variety of situations. Such happy days could not continue. Eventually I was forced to have my hair cut, my beard shaved, my flares and floral tie for court appearances were binned. And I was returned to what was regarded as normal CID police duties such as the prevention and detection of criminal acts - how sweet, but somewhat naive.

I am still not sure how the CID at Didsbury could be regarded as normal, but there I was, posted and clearly with much to learn, however brilliant I was in my own mind. The CID office had all the qualities of the squad room in the popular TV series, Hill Street Blues. Cramped conditions, old furniture, racing papers and the inevitable stench of goat curry and stale farts professionally blended with the hanging traces of Marston's Pedigree Bitter, direct from the Royal Oak, across the road. This establishment acted like a magnet from 11am onwards as it was viewed from the office window by many of us with aggravating symptoms of early alcoholism caused by never ending but fruitless periods of observations, usually but coincidentally in the officers' favourite haunt, the boozer.

Didsbury and beyond

My fate line continued to direct me, and I was confident that whatever happened, it was destiny and meant to be. I just went with the flow and when I was transferred to Didsbury Police Station, I did so without any argument. It was a type of promotion to permanent CID and I knew all about Didsbury from my Drug Squad days. Despite the relentless social life I had gained a reputation for many high profile arrests and now at least in my mind this was being recognized.

Didsbury Police Station was and still is a quaint little building with featured stonework framing an attractive style of brickwork. During my time in the CID office based there it was a hive of activity with the uniformed branch on the ground floor and CID on the first floor with even its own Detective Inspector.

As with most police stations there was a desk for the public to report their vast variety of complaints, all of which were noted, most ignored. But all, in the main, resulting in a satisfied 'customer' leaving the station in the albeit mistaken belief that their 'lost purse' was now a priority, to be treated with the identical level of gravity as a murder, which in truth all complainants believed with this relentless public relations exercise which over the passing years has deteriorated to the point where Sir Peter Fahy the present 2013 Chief Constable of

Greater Manchester Police has seen fit to give lessons to the existing plebs in good manners and public relations. The ink was hardly dry on this naïve little directive when Jordan Begley, only 23 years old, was confronted with a serving officer with a Taser, who because of disgraceful intelligence believed him to be a wanted criminal. The wrong man at the wrong time was approached in his own home, told to stand back despite having nowhere to go because of the kitchen table and was then Tasered and as a result died. Did we take any comfort from the IPCC investigating? We'll have to wait and see.

Didsbury had all the attributes of the city centre and the A Division. Women were everywhere and available under a variety of circumstances. I had always had deliberate limited success with policewomen, for a variety of reasons most relating to their reluctance to shag in the divisional van when the public at large revelled in such activities. I did however marry a policewoman during my uniformed service and remained wed for 24 years until the menopause and HRT took its toll and she decided she was 18 again and decided to shag the office car valet.

Even in 'civvies' it was a simple matter to engage with females on the division and move into their frilly underwear. As when in uniform, it was quite a simple matter to stop women driving home. Some of the plain cars had a blue 'Kojak' light and a flash of that reflected in their paling complexion had a dramatic effect. Some were married, and usually very drunk. The fact that their arrest was clearly not imminent, the colour returned to their complexion and further flushing as they became drunkenly amorous. There was no such thing as the breathalyzer, especially in the CID at this time, and enforcement of the law relating to drink driving was very relaxed in all areas of the police except for the traffic department. Flat white caps, bulging bellies and a smirking rolling swagger appeared to be part of this lowly position leaving many lives in ruins as they relentlessly breathalysed all that moved in a car with their new found powers. The more enlightened and forgiving officers of Manchester's finest found the enforcement of the drink driving laws could easily be adapted and performed, so to speak in the form of sexual favours, usually in the back seat of the offender's own car.

My successes in Didsbury were based on a similar uniformed experience in the city. On one occasion, I remember two females driving past a colleague and I. As we smiled and waved it was obvious just how pissed they were as they waved back. The driver didn't notice the Stop sign ahead. She passed over the white line and collided with a Post Office van which was hardly damaged. The postman was happy to leave his details and vacate the scene. Although very drunk, the driver was not impressed at being distracted. We wrote up the accident as "no fault" because the Stop sign was actually broken and it was not illuminated. Well, that was the case after we hurled a couple of bricks through the illuminated plastic casing. Instant fines followed. How should I put it? We were just two happy constables, carrying out their civic obligations with two model citizens, giving their best to the law. I actually saw the passenger on three other occasions until her husband stopped her coming home so late from town.

As with the city centre Didsbury had many quality retail establishments and as a consequence, female shop managers were also a favourite target. I had the pleasure to know a few and pleasure a few more. I suppose I knew many of them in a King James biblical sense as well. One such lovely, who I remember above all the others, managed a branch of a well-known national name that will remain anonymous. Many happy hours were spent during the evening patrol of Market Street after closing time, in the rear stockroom. As I have already alerted you, I was expected to wear my helmet, studded collar and tie, but nothing else. This seemed peculiar at this inductee stage in my sexual career, but it was no stranger than other lessons I was learning at the time. I came to accept the helmet bobbing sex, but perhaps lost a certain fondness for it in my later years as I moved into the CID.

She was eventually promoted to area manager and the stockroom was sadly no longer available. We then met at her home in Bolton and did so for many years. I think this wonderful arrangement floundered when my entrepreneurial ambitions were on the rise. I asked her if she would put me into a situation where I could purchase seconds of the clothing sold at the shop. It didn't happen. And neither did any more tremblers, but onwards and upwards in my new pastures.

Most of the sub-stations such as Didsbury did not have any cells and so there was no real stench of urine badly disguised with undiluted disinfectant in the ground floor of the building, nor any screaming or cell door banging to alarm the 'old ladies' of the suburb. Cell blocks in all police stations are often very noisy. The cell doors are heavy; they make a loud noise when closed especially with prisoners heads trapped in them. Bored prisoners incessantly kicked the cell door purely for something to do, that was until they were subjected to a similar kicking.

It is worth briefly describing the various adjoining divisions which were strictly policed as far as crime went, remaining within the many boundaries. Shagging was fair game anywhere in the city or even into the adjoining county forces, but pillaging of bars and restaurants was again a no no, reserved for the servants of the Queen on that particular division. Didsbury was known as the third section of four of the D Division. The D Division had its headquarters at Longsight Police Station, which was situated on Stockport Road only about four miles from the city centre and for a landmark, it is not far from where the Apollo Theatre is situated. At this time during the 70s the Longsight area was populated by the Irish labouring community to such a degree that it had an enormous Irish theatre club, a single storey building about the size of a cinema of the day. For those that know Manchester police divisions, the D Division ran from the A Division boundary where I completed my uniform service, plain clothes and some CID work, outward to the South bordering with the E division, which covered Moss Side, the Jamaican black area.

The D had Manchester Royal Infirmary and the then comparatively fledgling Manchester University, which now covers what must be five times the area it did back then. It travelled out through Longsight into Burnage - the birthplace of the fighting Gallaghers, the Oasis brothers Noel and Liam - and Levenshulme and on along the A34 where the 3rd section boundaries commenced. We covered some of Burnage, which is really a massive council estate, Withington, generally an area populated by students and nurses in bedsits. The new manor also housed the Christie Cancer Hospital, now with vivid memories of a very black period of my life when those I loved seemed to die one by one in such a short space of time.

The patch then ran from Withington, through a class housing area with some large impressive properties, where Richard Madeley and Judy Finnigan lived during their days in Manchester. Didsbury had Richard, who I like as a presenter, in the nick for allegedly helping himself to a couple of bottles of wine in Tesco at Parrs Wood, Didsbury. He was found not guilty apparently suffering a memory failure – many become forgetful having consumed the wine not usually while shopping for it. The division continued into quaint Didsbury village, which still has some quality bars and food establishments. Now it is a hive of eateries of all descriptions, quality food purveyors, some remaining from my days and still some large quality homes and wealthy residents. Didsbury has always had its own synagogue and so the Jewish community has always lived around this area. They maintain the standards and build an invisible barrier from the creeping body of Asians who are moving into the area.

They moved in to live and also buy the larger Victorian properties to convert to flats and rent out to students, who seemed to put up with any expensive crap. Didsbury was back then known as Yidsbury and was a target area for burglars strolling the short distance from Wythenshawe. The burglars saw these posh houses as easy targets, when taking a rest from shagging their sisters and even on occasions their mothers. Be in no doubt that during these times, the majority of the population on this sprawling estate were classic scrotes, whole families of them, who had been rehoused from council accommodation elsewhere in the city. The council decided their old accommodation was unfit for human occupation. The original houses must have been deplorable as these transient scrotes were the pits of humanity. They had no real moral compass, they had no family values and went through life existing from one crime to the next, be it burglary or shoplifting, or shagging their own mothers and children.

They even expected a good hiding whenever arrested whatever the circumstances. Their experience and knowledge of the police also allowed for an occasional good kicking just in passing, purely for disciplinary purposes. Whilst hardly PC it was an acceptable practice to 'keep the lid on' and it was great training just giving the wandering scumbag a severe hiding to keep your hand in. As with planting goods on passing suspected shoplifters, such a belting acted as a deterrent and had a dramatic effect. With the younger members such a crack at least forced them to think twice before entering the realms of criminality with any serious beliefs.

Still moving South(ish) the 3rd section changed to the 4th section which encompassed the largest council estate in Europe with all its problems, thefts, assaults, murders, burglaries and incest which was very popular with the perverted drunken louts fancying their own children. In reality these sick souls didn't know any better as their own father's often fiddled with them. Such crapheads as I have already related were rehoused from redeveloped areas throughout the city and they formed a nucleus of the population. However, many older and thoroughly decent people were moved to Wythenshawe, often under loud protest to be sprinkled amongst all this human rubbish without any consideration of the nightmares they were to experience living amongst them. The majority had never seen such human garbage.

A drive through Wythenshawe easily identified which houses were populated by each section of this disjointed community. Some of the houses had gardens, with bright flowers and mowed lawns, flowering tubs and hanging baskets finishing off the lovely appearance. The privet hedges were neatly trimmed and even the garden gate had had a coat of paint. Next door could easily have an uncut privet hedge, a flagged lawn area with the obligatory rotting mattress and rusting washing machine, probably replaced by Manchester Social Services, leaving the old items to be tipped by the householder. For many the front garden seemed an ideal tipping point and an instant playground for the children with no thought for the obvious dangers.

Of course, Wythenshawe also played host to the Golden Garter Theatre Club and whether we liked it or not we would run the gauntlet through the estate from Didsbury to the club in the hope we would not be asked to assist the resident troops on this section with removing a father from his daughter, or a suspicious cot death, an event which was too common in this area to be genuine all the time. Forensic tests which developed over the years improved considerably and later proved that cot deaths were murder in several instances either by the retarded mother, not fit to have children or the pissed-up father returning from a hard day in the Benchill pub and annoyed at the incessant crying.

The 4th section was based at Brownley Road Police Station, which was right in the centre of this seething mass of life's failures. This building was a post war red brick box, unattractive, again with its own busy public desk, cells and CID offices on the first floor. Unlike Didsbury it had its own charge office where arrests were charged and either held in the cells or bailed if actually living at a set address and appearing on the voters' register, which was always the key and strangely this was more often the case. Whilst such registering appears strange for such retards it was the case that they would not be able to claim any benefits unless properly registered as a resident on the voters' register.

The CID officers based at Didsbury, but working out of Brownley Road regarded us as non-working playboys and we all only met when they came out of the wilderness to drink in the Royal Oak, opposite Didsbury nick, having no real pub where they could relax in Wythenshawe.

At Didsbury, we had a better populace, a better class of villain and better pubs with a much better choice of women, often married, usually divorced, and many students who as today were indulging in prostitution just to make ends meet. As such a wanton sexual activity came to light, usually from a whistle-blowing neighbour we investigated, not because it was a criminal offence, which it was not, but out of a perverted interest. We were easily able to frighten the living daylights out of these lovely little things to the point of instant fines, an art honed from my days in uniform on the A Division. Back then street-walking prostitutes were often fined as they walked from one hostelry to the next. These impressionable little girls even got a kick from shagging a detective and often wanted to pose in a photo with their tame detective to show to their friends, which whilst great fun could have horrendous consequences.

Fingers in every didsbury 'pie'

Most offences on the 3rd section of the D Division consisted of burglaries and thefts from vehicles which were treated in a similar manner to the A Division. There was a standard procedure laid down throughout the force where all scenes of crime were visited, fingerprints attended, the complainants regularly updated on the telephone and with personal visits, which were a must in the climate of public relations. Each incident had its own crime number and individual crime report. This form was a work of art with many sections, titled and designed to ensure that all facets had been properly dealt with. Every visit and phone call was endorsed and recorded. Visits were made by the Fingerprint Department and where there had been a witness which was rarely the case, they would be taken to Longsight Criminal Records Office where they were shown volumes of photographs of previously convicted offenders. This was a strange practice because on many occasions, viewers recognized neighbours and colleagues, causing many embarrassing moments even resulting in dismissal in employer-staff incidents.

The CID work at Didsbury differed greatly to other divisions. All burglaries were visited and the scene properly examined. The Fingerprint Department attended and covered every flat surface with a white dust. Fingerprints were often found as many burglaries were committed by the drug-taking community, who also populated flats in some of the roads in Didsbury and then elimination fingerprints had to be taken of all members of the household to establish if there was a strange print. The print was then searched in the volumes of records with a system of recognition that I never really understood.

Until I heard of a particular murder being detected on fingerprint evidence and the culprit hanged, I didn't have much faith in the Fingerprint Department, believing it to be merely a public relations exercise. Whenever I visited complainants in their homes after the Fingerprint Department had attended the first point of conversation was how much time it had taken the householder to remove the white dust, but tempered with: "Well it's nice to see that every attempt is being made."

To say eccentricity reigned with a touch of the 'Enid Blytons' to achieve a realistic detection rate is an understatement, not by any particular individual, but the entire CID in general. I learned a great deal from the legendary senior officers of my times such as John Thorburn, Tom Butcher, Eric Jones, Roy Hartley, Charlie Horan, Douglas Nimmo, Arnie Beales, Callum McDonald and many more in the ranks below, despite my mild encounters from the other side of the fence.

The actual workers such as DI John Thorburn and DI Eric Jones were slowly replaced by the John Stalkers and much worse, the James Andertons, who luckily had been very few and far between during my service, but appear to abound in the present day policing. These are men who made an art of doing the minimum of sharp-end police work, fearing that their accelerated promotion would be badly affected by a complaint imposed by some scrote or other, fearing it would tarnish their impeccable record.

James Anderton when Chief Constable has to accept full responsibility for this ethic in Greater Manchester Police and the resulting general failure of the force during the later years of his service. It was during Anderton's reign that no-go areas became accepted in places such as Cheetham Hill, a secondary city area to be populated by ethnic minorities, and Moss Side, a large part of which was populated by West Indians. The detection rate dropped to abysmal reality and the streets of Greater Manchester were not safe to walk. Even fabricating TICs which maintained the detection rate became a tightrope and one not worthy of the risk. It grew like an understanding amongst the force that Anderton was not working, harassing the 'troops' with his headline-grabbing antics which became so many that it became general knowledge that the Home Office had told him to shut up. With such lame leadership why should the rest of us, the ones at the pointed end make any real effort?

As I have said, the CID offices looked like a set in Hill Street Blues and I wonder, sometimes, if plots for these programmes were taken from Manchester CID in general. The plots for Heartbeat and The Bill were certainly not. The general office had just about enough seating for us all, for morning parade. There were two side offices for interviews and a bit of quiet writing and the Detective Inspector's office, where it certainly felt like being on a daily roller coaster ride for the man in the hot seat. When I started, we had Inspector John Thorburn. I have mentioned him with great respect in previous chapters, and indeed he deserves the print. There were not enough like him. I can't say enough concerning him and those of his calibre. There were so few honourable names and so many counterfeits, that a little repetition is a forgivable offence.

John was a good man, a steady man, a real detective of the old school and a little too outspoken to proceed quickly up through the ranks of inexperienced YES men. As officers progressed through the force and their rank got higher, potential promotion candidates were interviewed by several senior officers on a Promotion Board. John only had to be asked: "What is wrong with the police today, Mr. Thorburn?" The usual and perhaps safe response might have been of the "Well run, but underfunded" school. But John Thorburn told the truth. The truth didn't help his promotion prospects. It hardly ever does. There were always other, higher criteria at stake. The truth, too many times, was a mere distraction, an impediment in the way of an imperfect justice.

John appeared quite content at Didsbury and enjoyed the six o'clock pint at the Royal Oak, which was conveniently opposite the station. He used this location to mildly discuss work, but in the main judged his men fairly and formed a type of working bond. He never came on the real piss-ups, unless it was to mark one of the office stalwarts leaving for greener pastures or civilian life depending on the circumstances.

'Tricky' Jack Butler didn't have time for a leaving do. He was arrested for a series of offences which so many serving detectives treated as the norm, but in reality, not to such extremes as Jack. He was jailed in 1983 at Manchester Crown Court for offences of corruption and brutality whilst a Detective Chief Inspector. He was sentenced to about seven years imprisonment, but served only about four. The fact an officer of such a rank could be investigated and charged with such offences highlighted to us all that the 'the times they were a changing' and 'there but for the grace of God go I.'

Jack Butler was a one-off. He took pride in being known as totally bent and a raging psychopath to boot. Where it was the norm to plant evidence, beat up prisoners and bribe informants to set up another criminal individual, Jack always went that bit too far and his treatment of prisoners and the beatings he gave them caused concern to real seasoned detectives. Jack's conviction and imprisonment sent ripples throughout the CID and eventually other matters he had dealt with where he had secured convictions were investigated and properly examined. This action was seen as a very alarming deviation from the norm where such behaviour had been accepted for so many years by the 'troops' on the ground, but supported by the senior supervisory officer ranks in their quest for the perfect detection figures. Once a successful investigation had been completed and filed away it was of course the unwritten rule that the file would remain closed. Jack's example was an alarming deviation from this practice and could have affected us all with other matters, but perhaps with less heart-stopping examples.

One such case which became known as the UK's longest running miscarriage of justice involved a man named Robert Brown who had the misfortune of being interviewed/tortured/beaten close to death....you choose, by 'Tricky' Jack Butler. He led the interview and worked with other officers who beat a confession out of Brown, which resulted in a signed statement confessing to a murder. Brown who was 20-years-old at the time was charged with the murder of Annie Walsh, a 51-year-old factory worker. As a result of Jack Butler's convictions for offences totally unrelated to the murder investigation, the Criminal Cases Review Commission found multiple grounds for doubts in the safety of Brown's conviction. They revealed that Jack's 1983 conviction related to crimes he committed in the 1973-5 time frame, pre-dating Brown's 1977 trial.

Of course the jury was not to know of Jack's activities and his reputation and was left only with the summing up of Mr Justice Milmo, who gave the jury the simple decision of believing the police or the accused whose only defence was the fact that his confession had been beaten out of him. The confession was found to be the 'chief plank of the case' by the Review Commission.

The conviction was found to be unsafe because of Jack Butler's conviction on the other unrelated matters. Brown was now found 'not guilty.' There is a great difference here. It must be remembered when pitying Brown for the 25 years he spent in jail before the Court of Appeal released him on November 13th 2002 that he was not just picked up off the street and charged with this offence. Evidence pointed to him, but it was not enough and his statement added the finishing touches. It must be asked, whether an innocent person would sign such a statement which would result in a life sentence and what did Butler have to gain by fabricating all the evidence without even a glimmer of truth. A murder such as this necessitated the use of many detectives and to suggest Butler was alone in the commission of this offence is ludicrous and itself, a serious omission. As with the Hillsborough conspiracy there were many officers of various ranks involved in this corruption of evidence and as time will tell only a few prosecutions if any at all will follow with the majority using the tried and trusted SS explanations of WWII: 'I was acting on orders' as has occurred in so many other such investigations.

What differs with the Hillsborough conspiracy is the fact that it is indeed a proven conspiracy which totally explodes the constant plea of a rogue element of a few people with values of yesteryear. Examine the proof to date which itself will cause some serious attempts at avoiding the truth in the final report by virtue of the ranks and numbers of conspirators. Consider the facts? There are already named four Chief Constables, four Superintendents, several members of the Police Federation, a Coroner, three Judges, two Members of Parliament and at least 200 uniformed police officers. The inquiry is dragging on, probably in the hope that the main suspects will die giving everyone someone to blame.

In the case of Brown and Jack Butler there was a statement for the media from the usual police spokesman after the appeal court judgment which said: "We would like to reassure the people of Greater Manchester that procedures under the Police And Criminal Evidence Act now provide safeguards for both suspects and officers." These include recording of the interview process and advanced forensic techniques. The public of Greater Manchester, as indeed the populace of the UK are still awaiting such promised and devastating improvements. Of course there have been some improvements as was inevitable, but equally so improvements have again been adapted by the servants of the Queen to their own needs and such corruption and violence continues on a daily basis. It is rarely publicized unless the victim is an MP as in the Plebgate incident.

The advanced forensic techniques glibly mentioned as a safeguard in the police statement also work against a defendant. It is now a simple procedure to transfer DNA of, say a murder victim, onto a suspect. Traces of gunpowder residue can be equally fabricated and transferred to a suspect's clothing in minute quantities in the knowledge that the much improved and professional forensic teams will undoubtedly find the 'proof.' For example, Barry George the alleged killer of Jill Dando was convicted on forensic evidence, but later released because of the unsatisfactory nature of various aspects of the police evidence. In refusing to award any compensation to George, the 'learned' Judges are continuing to disbelieve any suggestion of deliberately fabricated evidence. It is yet another example of the old judicial head in the sand syndrome developed from so many years of protected development ensuring that they never crossed paths with a drunken hairy-arsed detective or equally a Wythenshawe scrote, recently dismounting from his mother or sister.

Corruption at Manchester's Platt Lane police station in the 1970s centred on detectives who, were sharing in the proceeds of crime in the area, but an official police statement made no mention of criminal action being taken against any officers.

It was in the interests of nobody at this time to investigate the deep-seated practices of the CID and the fact that such corruption existed in every police station, throughout the city.

I enjoyed Jack Butler's company, especially when playing rugby for the force. Jack had a bald head despite his young years and with all the scarring from rugby or from prisoner "reform," the skin of his head looked like a map of spaghetti junction. He wasn't very big, but as with many men of his abbreviated size, was a deceptively nasty, little bastard and would do anything to gain the upper hand. On leaving prison he set up his own private detective agency. By then, I had left the police and had my own agency. To be modest, it was big and it was successful, with about 40 staff at this time. By that point, I was so pissed off with the ruination and conduct of the police that as earlier mentioned I used to specialize in employing men who had been sacked by the police and the armed forces for minor indiscretions, none of which involved dishonesty because they would have been discredited witnesses when appearing in court. I was always examining new staff applications. Jack's incarceration did certainly involve dishonesty I had no intention of having anything to do with his business, but we met anyway, for old time's sake. He asked for work. Nothing he said convinced me he was to be a good and loyal employee and, clearly, I was just to be a source of training for him before he went off on his own with all the invaluable experience and, maybe, a few of my clients as well.

It was only shortly after the meeting with Jack that I was invited to a party by Kevin Taylor - the Manchester businessman who found himself at the centre of the John Stalker affair. At the party was Stalker, the then Assistant/Deputy Chief Constable of Manchester, who in his book had the temerity to deny knowing me just to suit his own book sales and alter the public view of Mr Whiter than White which he most certainly was not. Stalker in his supercilious pontificating manner advised me to have nothing to do with Jack. I never would have done anyway, but based on my own assessments.

In the CID we all suffered varying levels of pressure of work, whatever the causes. There was certainly a large volume of crime reports which required investigating and our lives were often complicated with extra-marital activities, drinking and dining the pillaged wares of the section did not leave much time for family life. I had visited the scene of a particular burglary on several occasions. It was a big house, and as a consequence a great deal of valuable property had been stolen. This was real police work for real reasons and certainly did actually occur on so many occasions with all of us and perhaps much more than I have impressed in my accounts of so many 'bent' activities. Each time I visited, the house was unoccupied and I was unable to take the fingerprints of the householders for elimination purposes. I was very busy with other matters and there was only so much time I could give to this particular matter. I had a couple of naughty little students to visit, the Royal Oak to meet the lads, Ken Dodd was on at the Golden Garter, what could I do?

Eventually, I completed the form with my own prints and submitted the file as complete. This of course was rumbled and wasted everyone's time at the Fingerprint Department. As a result I was threatened with all sorts of disciplinary procedures if I ever repeated such a heinous offence. Of course I had submitted the prints due to 'pressure' of work and the fact that the householders were never at home whenever I visited. I was impressed by this detection of my own stupidity.

As I have said, I had always believed that the Fingerprint Department was merely a public relations exercise, so to identify the prints of a serving police officer was quite surprising. What I didn't know was that my prints were so unusual that they were used as examples in teaching scenarios and courses and for the fingerprint aficionados my prints were the equivalent of a famous film star and apparently recognized anywhere in the world.

Visiting burglary scenes introduced a different type of female into my perfect little debauched world. The complainants, married, single, or students, all needed a little reassurance that an intruder hadn't been sniffing their underwear drawer, or masturbating in their gloves, which sometimes happened. Some burglars even defecated in the bed. I always thought this was some sort of perversion but, having asked such a perpetrator, I was told they were so nervous they just dropped it anywhere they were at the time. If they were going through the dressing table, in the bedroom, then it was the bed so that they could wipe their arse on the sheets.

The reassurance I was offering to these women sometimes led to a little cuddle, a kiss on the forehead, all, of course, for support. It rarely led to a fondle of the breasts and general undressing, that is, until the second follow up call when the shock of the burglary had gone with the installation of a new alarm system. The alarm had often been provided by a good company, advised by the visiting officer and the necessary commission paid by the grateful company, totally stepping around the divisional crime prevention officer who was also seeking his kickback. Every division had its own crime prevention officer and indeed such a position exists today. They were a law unto themselves and dutifully visited every burglary. The CID officer yet again filled in their little box on the crime report accumulating the proof of action points, eventually resulting in the division's answer to the Blue Peter badge which was the signing off of the paperwork as yet another statistic, an unsolved crime, waiting to be written off at a later date by a clerical exercise known as a TIC, which stands for Taken Into Consideration.

When a prolific thief or burglar was arrested the 'friendly detective' caring and wishing the best for this young man, explained that all the offences he was suspected of committing previous to his arrest would now be investigated by all the CID on the division and that he would become a priority investigation. It was explained that whatever sentence he got for the arrested offence, would pale into insignificance with the numerous added charges in the future and indeed if he got a suspended sentence he would then be immediately rearrested and the sentence of imprisonment would be imposed.

The prisoner's new best friend explained that this was to be his chance to 'clear the decks' and start afresh. With such a simple ruse and the fact that the prisoner was not aware that the local women, the Royal Oak and the Golden Garter actually took priority, he was inevitably tricked into admitting other offences with which he would not be charged. Being brainless scrotes they really believed that if they admitted all they had done they would not be pursued for other matters and 'the slate' would be cleared. Should they not do so it was stressed that they could be rearrested on leaving prison, if imprisoned or if not pulled out of the pub any Friday night.

In stupidly believing this, the happy villain, confident that his caring officer was looking after his welfare, would sign a statement to the effect that he had committed say, 30 burglaries over a 12 month period and in doing so had travelled throughout Manchester and Cheshire. Now therein lies the problem. There is no value in detecting burglaries in Cheshire, or on another division, as they would benefit from the detection in their figures and not the arresting officers of Didsbury. We couldn't have that and so we selected the 30 from our division. They were all undetected crimes with no chance of success. The boss knew the story and all 30 were stamped up as TICs with a red rubber stamp that was kept in his drawer.

Through the following months they would be fed into the system and passed through the statistics department, who were apparently oblivious to this deception and again Enid triumphed in yet another way. Each section of every division had a constant detection rate and the TICs in the boss' drawer were there to bump up the figures in a bad month.

The A Division in the city centre always had the best rate because of all the shoplifters, who again were adopted by a new friend and as a result also admitted other offences but in a greater volume. Each shoplifted item was treated as a single crime and where a house had been searched many items were inevitably recovered. The prisoner would be charged with two specimen charges and the remainder accepted as TICs. This entire system was condoned from the top and as corroboration one only has to consider the fact that there was even a special form printed by the force printers with its own reference number. This form was filed with the two specimen charges, but never actually sent on to the statistics department as they would then have refused to allow all the crimes to be treated separately. The statistics department must have been vaguely aware that they were being tricked and that the detection rate was being adjusted. Occasionally, they would look out for a mass of TICs from the same prisoner and insist on them being treated as the same detection as the two charges, but they could not trace them all if fed through the system over a period of weeks and months. The injection of poor leadership, men who had never seen an angry man, or even made an arrest, was causing serious moral issues amongst the rank and file. These so called leaders had no idea of reality out 'in the field' and should an officer be found to have cocked up evidence, or beaten a confession out of a thieving scrote, the arresting officer would be investigated and often with dire consequences. The days of planting, verballing evidence, tampering and the like were coming to an end.

The old stalwarts attempted to ignore the not too subtle changes to what was expected of their conduct in protecting and serving Joe Public. The sharp practices ground to a halt and with them the detection rate plummeted and as a result the bosses decided that some further detection ingenuity was required to keep the public happy. A detective constable on each division was given the duty of visiting prisons and discussing further admissions with prisoners who were again subjected to the same script of being met at the gates on release. Such admissions were again treated in a similar manner to TICs and again the detection rate blossomed and the boss was happy. Again, a special form was printed for this further crime rate deception. Very few crimes are actually detected by good old fashioned investigations, enquiries, door knocking, witnesses and great reliance is placed on the villains being caught at the scene, or selling the property later. It is from such arrests that the fabricated confessions were developed and in turn this maintained the good old detection rate, which was and maybe still is for that matter, later published for public consumption in the annual, 'aren't we doing well' report which of course was written with similar flair to the Hillsborough, Jimmy Savile and the miners' strike reports.

In the present day police force where thousands of frontline men are being made redundant to save money the crime rate is continually shown as dropping as related earlier in the introduction. Of course, this is impossible and again the present day statistical Enid Blytons must be at work.

Visits to crime scenes often led to romantic little meals, with the female householder. Starting as a friendly snack on the breakfast bar, with the ladies, when their hubbies worked away but, sometimes and more often than you would ever imagine, progressing to a trembler over the same breakfast bar. One of the sergeants with whom I regularly worked was a legend in his own right, charming, mischievous sparkling eyes, but a smiling assassin with many unbelievable stories to his credit. He had three regular ladies, whom he rotated so to speak which worked very well for him, most of the time as I was able to cover for him as we invariably worked together with some success. Unlike most of us, being such a nice guy and perhaps not wishing to 'look a gift horse in the face' he was unable to say enough is enough and trim off the surplus ladies in his note book, servicing them all through a working week. It all worked like a well-oiled machine, well it would with the baby oil, liberally used to accommodate the older lady he favoured, who perhaps was having difficulty with the natural lubrication. That is until Christmas when he had obligated himself to three Christmas dinners, so that he didn't upset anybody, in addition to the one at home. I'm not sure whether his active sex life was the issue on Christmas Day as time must have been an additional issue. It took a lot of nerve to simply hold the social aspect together. I never understood how he managed to convince his wife he had been picked to work Christmas Day, year after year and how on earth could he eat the dinner at home after so much food consumed during his earlier visits!

Of course we really did attempt to detect various crimes and actually showed some considerable success. In the main they are boring to relate, but in addition to so many 'run of the mill' offences we investigated on a daily basis there were always some that seized the imagination of the investigating officer. There were a variety of reasons, which themselves involved the need for the introduction of some evidence just to 'tidy' the job up or 'fill the gaps.' These measures if not properly planned, out of familiarity and the total disregard for any real official investigation could cause a level of twitching of the officer's nether regions should a 'wheel appear to have come off' with the chain of evidence. After all he was a member of 'The Biggest Gang In Britain' and in the end had no one to really answer to, but despite this in a manner of speaking 'the books had to be straight.'

Complaints were generally brushed under the carpet provided the offence by the officer was not so bad it could not be lied about. Caught bang to rights was the popular term. Of course even with investigations as serious as Hillsborough it was a simple matter to write around the 96 deaths and relax in the knowledge that the carefully-crafted words would be accepted. As the Independent Police Complaints Commission became a feature it was soon common knowledge that it was only the police investigating the police, but in another guise and no real action would be taken once the various avenues of possible criticism had been properly covered. Even today the IPCC is staffed by ex-police officers who complete the 'donkey' work before reporting to their 'civilian leaders' who again are deceived by the contents of the final report. Even before the IPCC has any form of report, officers actually serving in the same force as the officer complained about have juggled the facts with their initial reports.

This kind of thing happened during the 70s and remains so today, a culture of dishonesty and fabrication. An investigation by the Political Editor of the Daily Mail, James Chapman, during 2012 established that there were actually 1,000 serving police officers, found guilty of a variety of crimes. These were not petty crimes. Seventy-seven had convictions for violence, 36 had convictions for theft. Other offences covered a broad spectrum, including perverting the course of justice, kerb-crawling, benefit deceptions, robbery and even supplying unclassified DVDs. It's no surprise to see that the Biggest Gang In Britain still operate as the law outside the law like they did in my days in the force.

They Meant Well...Really

The theft of a large sum of cash was the basis for one particular investigation. It was very interesting to the bent brigade in the CID because of several intriguing factors. It was a common form of entertainment for all the CID to watch with perverted glee as somebody or other squirmed and hung on to their job by their fingertips after 'skating very close to the wind.' Nearly being found out could have very dramatic consequences. Then having skated so close to dismissal, those who wriggled and cajoled their way out of the mire would suddenly dive straight back into the same corrupt cesspool. Only now they had the added knowledge and what could only be seen as an education from avoiding what caused the difficulty in the first place. Such an education then ensured that a similar cesspool could be avoided in the future.

Before I go any further I have to confess I had nothing to do with this very entertaining incident, which became general common knowledge and revered as a 'there but for the grace of God go I' incident by the entertained rank and file. The actions by the detectives involved were in keeping with normal working practices and generally accepted procedures throughout the ranking structure of practical working policemen. Of course it does not follow that the practices were honest and in keeping with the many notes of guidance carefully prepared for every contingency. Such practices did however stop abruptly at the graduates and college diplomas, struggling with yet more basic everyday issues of police leadership in the ill-fitting guise of pretending to be knowledgeable and efficient leaders of real men.

In this particular investigation, a suspect was apprehended with a substantial amount of cash and he could not explain how it came to be in his possession. Eventually, the funds ended up as the main exhibit in a prosecution for a bank robbery. A few additions such as added forensics and verbals were included to ideally tidy up the loose ends of the case. Immediately the officer involved in the arrest(s) recognized that even the villain did not know the exact total and therefore took what he regarded as his commission in what he saw as a Robin Hood scenario. Similar thinking to the MPs of recent times, where yet another smaller but much more powerful gang had decided to adapt the Theft Act to their own purposes. The large sum of cash was deposited in what was fondly known as the Property Room, where all exhibits involved in arrests and awaiting a trial were stored in numerical order and entered in a large journal, often with the briefest of descriptions.

A large amount of cash would be shown only as CASH, with no total for the reasons becoming obvious as I write. The initial little bung would be taken at the time, but very soon would be spent and this neatly stacked pile of readies would from then onwards play on the poverty-stricken minds of the arresting officer and his 'pals' as a possible source of income. As the end of the month neared, they "borrowed" some of the exhibit and replaced it later when paid, clearly believing that too much out, too soon could raise questions and felt the final bung would be better removed after the trial.

The everyday economic disasters were part of each detective's life and whilst providing for the family with their house, nice cars and the kids schooling the standard of living was constantly threatened by their inevitable socializing, gambling, cards, roulette and general married life expenditure. Such strains caused the need for further foraging into the Property Room and the anonymous looking envelope, where further small but increasing amounts were withdrawn, but again repaid later despite the increasing difficulty to do so. As months passed by, the need for financial support continued unabated and the exercise was to be repeated on several occasions. As the month end loomed and the temptation for the easy way out grew, so did the need to replenish the funds especially leading up to the trial, often a year later, but always leaving the total as was when deposited. There was no question that any of the money was taken 'with the intention to permanently deprive' as the Theft Act so ably dictates. Well that was until the end of the trial, when the figures would be adjusted as that deposited less the officer's pillage. The continual borrowing eventually led to an impossible balancing of the books as the figure 'borrowed' could not be returned in full and as the months marched on the gap widened. A small bank loan then proved necessary to balance the Property Room books. A spiral of complications were on the horizon though yet to magnify in a manner which was worthy of a tragedy but treated as a comedy by their CID colleagues looking on with unbridled amusement. Once consumed with jealousy the onlookers, in the privileged knowledge of the scenario were now really pleased that they were not privy to the regular loans despite being in a similar poverty-stricken position.

At the trial, the full amount of money was in place, nicely bagged in clear plastic for easy viewing, tidily labelled and numbered as one of the now many exhibits, some discovered in the investigation and some added to fill a small gap in the evidence. For continuity, which is vital with the seizure and storage of exhibits, the arresting officer stated that he had seized the money, sealed it, and labelled it in the exhibit bag that was now proudly presented before the court. He stated this on oath and by now committing perjury, which is a serious offence involving telling lies on oath in a court or at least in a legal environment. He told how the sealed exhibit bag had remained in the Property Room under locked and secure conditions until the day of the trial from the day of arrest. In what can only be regarded as a stroke worthy of Perry Mason, the wheelchair bound American defence lawyer of 70s television, the prisoner's solicitor had noted the numbers of several bank notes seen through the clear plastic covering and for a reason still not clear, but certainly very clever, had asked the Bank of England for the date of manufacture of the notes. The 'borrowing' of money and then replacing it was unheard of. Large sums of money, firearms, drugs and jewellery were often being taken, but this movement of the cash was really unheard of. The taking of money was fair enough, counting the money in court and finding the total to be lacking, yes, but not this honesty without a victim other than the evidence continuity procedures. The prosecution evidence was given first, over a couple of days and all looked lost for the prisoner. All went smoothly, all the evidential gaps had been filled and most of the jury were awake. The theatricals by both barristers were as expected.

The evidence was given and then challenged regarding various aspects. Several elements were inevitably challenged, because certain 'gaps' in the evidence had been filled and there was a little assistance from Enid in relation to the interview after arrest. Such cross examination was expected and the various witnesses came and went, but out of the blue, the prisoner's barrister recalled the arresting officer who had earlier been dispensed with during the first couple of days. The barrister produced a very impressive letter from the Bank of England and even signed by the name of the time, identical to that which appeared on every bank note. Very impressive, but for the officer clutching the sides of the witness box, somewhat and immediately alarming as he knew that he was about to get rumbled in full public view with nowhere to hide. Only ex-police of the day will recognize the feeling in the pit of the stomach with bowels twitching and cold sweats all professionally hidden behind the façade of concern for the necessary honesty of the moment. The official and impressive looking letter of only a few lines, gave stark proof of the dates of printing of the notes which were visible through the clear plastic. The letter proved that the notes had not even been printed at the time of the offence, let alone the date of arrest a few weeks later. Some of the notes had been printed many months later whilst the prisoner was on remand, in custody and as the entire prosecution file was so meticulously being prepared.

The file itself was immaculate. All the statements filled every requirement of the need for continuity in every area. The victim's representative had related the full details of the robbery. The Fingerprint Department gave evidence of their relentless search of thousands of filed prints and produced very large photographs of the print found at the scene compared with the tidier version, taken under controlled conditions. Each similarity had been arrowed for ease and there were many. The arresting officers gave details of observations, the arrest and interview at the police station with the cash exhibit. The fact that the money had been sealed in the clear plastic bag and labelled was laboriously related. The fact that it had been recorded and placed in the secure Property Room gave those in court the impression that it resembled a large walk in safe, but it was actually a large cupboard type room, unsuitable as an office with a basic mortise lock for security. All this amazing efficiency was expertly related, but to no avail.

Armed with the Bank of England letter the defence barrister with his usual theatrical flair was now brimming with contempt as he slowly rose from his seated position. "Officer..." he bellowed and then proceeded to relate the evidence of the dates of issue in the form of a speech rather than a cross examination. Even the judge was amazed and allowed the performance, the jury members were all wide awake and the entire court sat in a hushed silence. The barrister submitted the full account to the court and produced the evidential letter to the judge as the shamed officer appeared to shrink in the witness box. He was looking around for a friendly face for support, but nobody, not even his co-conspirator who had also had a 'taste' of the spoils, was looking his way. His pal now had his eyes firmly fixed on the floor as he sat in the rear of the court, which was by now feeling very much like a gallows.

The learned judge agreed with the theatrical defence performance and threw out the entire prosecution purely because of the blatant lies involving the evidence continuity. The officer had actually lied on oath and in doing so had committed perjury, a serious offence in the eyes of the naïve law. The learned judge clearly a supporter of corrupt police evidence whatever the circumstances questioned the officer how such a situation could occur and happily accepted the explanation, which clearly couldn't be true and involved a pile of money falling to the floor from a couple of cash arrests whilst the money was being further secured and listed. In the climate of 'get them done' today the property records would have been examined for the fictitious money introduced into the tale and of course in its absence the officer would once again be hauled before the judge who would have undoubtedly accepted yet another dubious explanation. It just wasn't done to prosecute the hard working police whatever corruption of the truth in the interests of 'justice' they may have pulled.

Whether judges were actually stupid enough to believe all police evidence, I just don't know, but they inevitably helped officers suffering in particularly hard-fought cross examinations only to get the conviction if they fancied the sentencing. This was such a case, the judge only publicly admonished the jabbering and quivering officer as he considered the inevitable, a strong term of imprisonment. The circumstances were referred to the CID hierarchy who clearly regarded it as yet another example of 'there but for the grace of God' and returned the officer to his usual duties with the intention of 'going straight.' This loosely interpreted as never getting caught again and no action was taken against him and of course he was not sacked. Yet again the 'Biggest Gang' was doing what they did and indeed do today, looking after their own.

Whilst a trifle out of context in my checkered career, the following story is worth the mention on the subject of permitted perjury, condoned by the judiciary and allowed to fly under the legal 'radar.' This concerns an officer with the rank of sergeant who was in fact the brother of a serving Detective Superintendent. I knew this man from my early cadet days. I knew his brother, who is older, from the CID at Bootle Street. Being a seasoned detective he was active in all that occurred at Bootle Street and was also an excellent detective with a proven prisoner interview technique.

When I left the police, I joined a private detective agency as a director. The wonderful title, actually meant nothing, as everyone was a director and operated in a similar manner to the Mexican Army where everyone is a General. I was contacted by a solicitor who had a client who had been arrested for importuning for an immoral purpose in a gent's toilet in Stockport. Clearly I was, by now, well known for liking the smell of stale urine blowing in my nostrils from my early days at Bootle Street and must have been thought perfect for this investigation. The solicitor was not hopeful of a defence, because his client, when arrested, was found to be wearing lady's underwear; including stockings, suspenders and cami-knickers. My reputation was such that if I could "cock-up" evidence so expertly when arresting such heinous 'offenders,' then I could also come up with a defence, whatever the weight of evidence. His co-accused had already pleaded guilty, but that fact did not mean our client was himself guilty. The client was married. He was also legally aided, but he wished to pay an extra £500 if he was found not guilty. This would ensure his wife did not find out about the arrest and that I might try harder to ensure his acquittal.

The toilets concerned were a single storey building with only four urinals and no cubicles. The building was at the roadside and at the rear the land fell away immediately down a hill. There were no windows, but high up in the wall, at the rear which faced the urinals, was an air vent with a metal grille. The grille was only about three inches deep and 18 inches wide. The actual wall in which the grille was set was about 12 inches deep with the grille set in the centre. This being the only means of ventilation, except for the entrance, obviously accounted for the strong ammonia laden stench. Immediately, I recognized this with fond memories of my Plain Clothes days. Such an essence could arouse a superb erection for those of that persuasion. Despite several perverted tastes this lingering aroma actually did nothing for me.

The evidence offered by the sergeant cited that he had looked through the grille at the rear of the building into the toilet and could clearly see the client with an erection standing back a little from the stall so that the other man, who was in a similar sexually aroused state, could see the exposed member. A normal course of events dictated they would then masturbate each other in the toilet, which always had the danger of a straight member of the public coming in and spoiling this little piece of romance, or to avoid such a scenario the two men leaving the toilet and performing in the car together. The caring sergeant decided to make his arrest during the foreplay and 'flag waving' stages and they were both charged with importuning for an immoral purpose. On visiting the toilets I could see that the evidence was, pardon the pun, "a cock-up." The evidence had been totally fabricated and should I prove this, the underwear and the lover's guilty plea would mean nothing.

The toilet had a high ceiling. On the inside, the vent in the wall was about seven feet from the floor. The urinals were about four feet from the wall. Had the sergeant looked at the rear of the toilets where he claimed to have made his observations, he would have seen that due to the land falling away at the rear, the vent was actually 10 feet above ground level and even then there was no foot hold due to the gradient. The size and position of the grille and the thickness of the wall meant that he would have had to look through the grille from above to give him the angle to look down at the stalls. He would also have had to have been over 10 feet tall. At five feet, eight inches, he was one of the smallest in Greater Manchester Police at the time. He had made no mention of using a ladder in his statement of evidence. Not only that, he had not been to the rear of the toilet and seen the difficulty, always relying on the usual guilty plea by the prisoner which ensured the minimum of embarrassing publicity with a small fine if any at all. It was of course common accepted practice to expect such a plea of guilty and many evidential formalities were avoided, purely for ease or perhaps this is best described as laziness.

Feeling sure we now had a strong defence, provided the ladders didn't appear in evidence as an afterthought, I decided to draw a plan of the toilets, showing all the measurements and proving it was impossible to observe through the vent unless your name was Gulliver. Having achieved an O level in Building Construction at Ducie Technical High School for boys, I was able to take all the measurements and produce scale drawings of the plan and elevation of the toilet, particularly showing a cross section of the rear wall. The height of the observing officer paled into insignificance, because I was able to prove that however tall the officer, he could not have seen inside the toilet, at least not at the necessary depth of the room, the height necessary to make any observation of the prisoner's genitalia. Because of the thickness of the wall, a straight line from the highest point outside would pass through the vent but in avoiding the wall on the inside, would only strike the client in the area of his chest. Therefore, unless he had a penis with extraordinary and enviable length, the entire evidence had clearly been fabricated.

Usually the arresting officers sat in a vehicle outside the toilets. Then, when two or more men had remained in the toilet for a period of time significantly longer than the average pee, the officers would enter quietly, being able to see only a split second of the activity. This was usually insufficient for evidential purposes, unless the officer had joined in as the coy interloper. I am afraid his Scottish sense of humour didn't allow for this. Clearly this was such a case, and as one was not giving the other a blow job, as sometimes occurred, the evidence, therefore, had to be given more than a mild touch of the Enid Blyton's and totally fictionalised to assist.

The client was found not guilty. In those days, magistrates found everyone guilty and bent over backwards to do so, whatever the evidence, usually because they owed a favour to the officer in the case (having been caught staggering from a nightclub previously, drunk driving or something similar). They must have regretted having been left with no alternative but to render the decision they did. Even then they didn't criticize the officer, despite the fact he had committed blatant perjury. As far as I am aware, no action was ever taken. Why should it? It was only a case of "there but for the grace of God go I." Having been found not guilty, the client decided he had been too generous with his £500 offer and refused to pay. Shortly after that, "some lousy bastard" showed the client's wife the file of evidence – funny old world. Today, with the naive seniority that exists the services of the 'hard working' officer would be dispensed with, but even today he would be allowed to resign rather than be charged with the offence.

The need for additional cash to supplement the meagre wages was a constant concern with the rank and file, out there at the pointed end, continuing to perform their duties with a variety of efficiency levels, but in conclusion, doing their best for Queen and country. There was always an angle in every situation that would lead to an earner. It just had to be recognized and developed and therein lies the skill.

The CID had more opportunities than most and in their ranks were officers attached to specific CID departments such as the Regional Crime Squad, the Stolen Vehicle Squad and even Murder Squads as and when they were formed. The weekly visits to suspect car dealers and scrap metal dealers were a nice little earner and from such visits grew a 'working' relationship. The suspect businesses were permitted to trade on with their clocked cars, changed number plates and masses of stolen metal provided that they put some information 'into the pot' in addition to the weekly bung. Such businesses were also a clearing shop for stolen property and often the out buildings were crammed with stolen spirits and electrical goods from a recent burglary. They could not risk aggravating the officers in case they returned with a search warrant and the cosy relationship continued on that basis.

The thefts of large amounts of such property, either from warehouses or truck trailers were common. Car dealers, upset by the fact that the property from such an enterprise had not been offered to them often shopped that particular enterprise to their 'tame' officer. The insurance companies would offer rewards for recovery and conviction of the guilty parties. Such rewards were very generous and it was the usual practice for the officer in charge of such a detection, successful only because of the information from the snout, to attend at the insurance company and collect the reward on behalf of the informant - who wished to 'remain anonymous' whether he did or not.

Whilst having many such successful conclusions, the insurance companies in their usual search for any petty get-out clause, decided that the need for anonymity on the part of the informant could save them a few quid and insisted that they hand the cash direct to the informant himself, giving some clerical directive from above as the reason, but in the knowledge that some informants would never step into the reward spotlight.

Informants were villains; they would not pass on the reward to the officer. In the past it was the practice to keep most of the reward and hand the snout a small amount claiming that was all that was available. The truth of this scam would soon be apparent and the 'loyal informant' would actually see the amounts really involved. This could not be allowed. A notorious very slippery yet highly amusing member of one of the squads decided on a full frontal attack.

He made an appointment for the informant to attend alone at the insurance company, claiming pressure of work and court commitments. On the day in question he visited a lady friend at Granada Television makeup department who he convinced to totally change his appearance for a police observation. Kitted out with a wig, a wild beard, black teeth a false prosthetic nose, complimented with built-up shoes he attended at the insurance firm's offices in sunglasses and a hat. He was not recognized and signed for the reward. Another day and yet another nice little earner, where there's a will there's a way as they say.

Judges were always finding excuses for the police dishonesty of the day. In their mistaken belief that they were supporting the hardworking police they have allowed, over the years for an uncontrollable body of men to come to expect that they can adapt and bend the law at a whim with little fear of any dire consequences. The Hillsborough conspiracy, the so called investigation into Cyril Smith MP, a practicing paedophile, and of course Jimmy Savile, the 'uncle' to so many children are all typical examples, allegedly all once again being investigated in a seemingly never ending pantomime. As with Norman Bettison, the Chief Constable of Hillsborough fame, offending officers are allowed to resign and disappear before any prosecution, however serious the offence. Bettison is actually accused of leading the writing off of 96 deaths as self-inflicted rather than embarrass friends guilty of yet more police inefficiency.

A typical example of alternative justice is that of an officer moved to the CID at Didsbury having been transferred from the Moss Side area as a result of a minor miscarriage of justice. Moss Side was a notorious area for prostitution and with that wonderful trade came the ponces. These are men who claim to protect the girls and in doing so take money from them. In reality they are supervised, beaten up and generally abused to keep the 'protector' in the manner he was accustomed. In Moss Side the majority of ponces were Jamaican, not known for their hard work ethic and tending to favour drug dealing and prostitution as their chosen career. The circumstances of this particular example of 'The Enids' should have involved a lengthy period of observations on both the ponce and his girls, but didn't for various reasons. A detailed picture would be built of the girls parading for business, one going off in a car with a male punter to return a relatively short time later to continue plying their trade. At this point the ponce would appear and money would change hands.

When repeated several times over several days, the case for living off immoral earnings was built. Of course actual cash could not be seen, but the evidence was adjusted to him counting the notes in full view rather than sliding the cash into his pocket. It always assisted the evidence if the ponce resided with the prostitute. During the alleged observations the home addresses would be identified and with a few well-chosen words the residence of the two would be proved. Such a lengthy period of observations certainly interrupted the social life and editing of the truth became necessary in certain areas of evidence. However the officer concerned with this particular little fabrication took it all too far. He spent a couple of nights establishing the basic movement patterns and then adjourned to a local hostelry, sometimes over a period of days running into weeks. Such evidence certainly relies a great deal on fabrication and has to rely a great deal on a touch of the 'Enid Blytons' and in some instances it is downright fiction from start to finish.

With regard to this matter, the officer was certainly over-enthusiastic with the added fiction even to the point of stressing how well he knew the subject and so identification could not be an issue. The officer had decided that the Jamaican brother was taking the piss and now it was 'his turn.' This was a common attitude which reigned at this time among hard working officers in the mistaken belief that any evidence would do to 'get them off the streets.' The evidence in this case was totally fabricated for no gain whatsoever and basically in the service of Her Majesty, purely to keep her highways and byways safe to walk.

In short, he had totally made up the evidence and written his statement perhaps in the vault over a couple of pints of Guinness. The evidence was perfect, but as the arrest was attempted the subject was nowhere to be found. This was not unusual and all he had to do was await his return to the area before arresting the subject, who was hysterical to say the least. In all such cases the arrested individuals never considered what they had previously done, without detection and certainly did not want to 'take one for the team.'

In yet another rare Perry Mason moment as the case came to court, his smirking 'arsehole' of a barrister produced a medical report. Now it was prepared by

Wythenshawe Hospital proving that his client was actually residing on a ward with his leg in traction having been badly broken in another arrest for a totally separate incident away from the Moss Side area, which occurred some days earlier than the period of evidence in relation to the proposed charge of living off immoral earnings. In addition to the charge which initiated the arrest the 'ponce' was also charged with police assault the age old standby to account for any injuries received either during the arrest and especially in the rear of the police van as he was being transported rather noisily to Platt Lane Police Station. Of course this station was on the same division as Moss Side, but inter sub-division intelligence was not what it is supposed to be today and the arrest never raised any other alarm bells on the E Division which was actually situated close to Maine Road football ground, the then home of Manchester City Football Club.

These were the days of outright colour prejudice, unabated and doled out in the form of violence on any passing unfortunate of the wrong colour. This man had put up a fight, was thrown to the ground and his leg stamped upon as it lay across a kerbside. Apparently he never complained in the knowledge that such a complaint would be ignored as the injuries were justified with a police assault charge.

Of course the production of the medical certificate caused a mild ripple of the bowels for the officer. The evidence of seeing the man on numerous occasions, taking money from prostitutes when he was in fact in hospital was certainly perjury once again and yet again there was no investigation as the court readily accepted the officer's limp explanation. "Well, he is black and it was night." And then: "I had to park some distance away to remain unseen." And the clincher: "I knew the woman to be under his control, and when I saw the man punching her, I knew it was him. I had seen him do this before."

Of course the bosses knew the truth, they had probably done similar. The officer was moved out of that division, where his duty was actually only a uniformed officer but in what is known as the Plain Clothes Department. Yet in recognition of his endeavours, however suspect, even illegal, he was moved up the invisible ladder to the CID. Get done and get on was always a popular phrase at this time in the police and there are many examples.

One such which comes to mind was the armed escort for the delivery of bank notes to the Bank of England, which then was situated near to Albert Square in a side street in Manchester. The cash was packed into trunk sized metal boxes and there were at least 20 of them. They were delivered to Piccadilly Railway Station by a train specially adapted for the delivery, with windowless carriages. The train was given priority into the farthest platform, which was nearest to the roadway exit used by the taxis and even private cars for dropping off in those days.

The British Rail van, an innocuous seven tonner of dubious reliability and age was driven onto the platform and the metal trunks were quickly loaded into the rear. At the entrance to the platform, from the public area were parked our Mini Coopers all shiny white and marked up as police cars. In each one was an advanced uniformed driver and an armed detective. Such armed detectives were also placed on the platform itself to view the unloading, but not to join in with such manual labour. Don't be silly.

Other police cars monitored the traffic lights and in fact the security was well beyond that allowed for HRH when he regularly visited Salford University. It was probably believed that the CID escort would lift the loot and therefore allocating such numbers would inevitably mop up a few honest ones who would prevent such a heist.

The convoy of the railway van with Mini Coopers back and front and also at the sides as it passed through the four lanes of Piccadilly, which was one way and then two way as it passed the imposing Piccadilly Hotel built several storeys above street level, above shops and Piccadilly Radio, latterly Key103, and the breeding ground of several DJ's later to move on up. Even to the dizzy heights of Radio 1 in the case of Andy Peebles and that chap Chris Evans of Radio 2 fame along with Channel 4's Big Breakfast Show and a heap of other celebrity drivel. Peebles had a great DJ voice, but when he presented Top of the Pops it was instantly apparent that he most certainly had a face for radio. And some say Evans wasn't much better with his glasses and ginger hair, but I quite like him.

The convoy would trundle on down a few side streets, secured by the police cars until the bank was reached. Pre-arranged calls were made and the rear doors opened immediately as the convoy arrived and the van disappeared up the ramp and inside.

Of course, a perfect example of smooth police efficiency, coordinating what was a perfect security exercise without a hitch. That is until on one occasion, the convoy was just about to enter the four lanes of

Piccadilly when a CID man, an Inspector as I recall was spinning his gun on his finger in true cowboy style. When the gun went off, it did so without any control and could have easily shot the driver, fired through the floor or even the engine with an inevitable ricochet that could have gone anywhere. By an unbelievable stroke of luck the bullet passed through the roof, making a neat round hole in the lining, but a jagged exit as it passed through the thin metal, still rather neat in a modern artistic way but noticeable, especially if it rained. Options of fitting an extra dummy ariel were considered along with stuffing a few roses in the hole as an alternative.

The uniformed driver was not keen, he knew he had come within an inch of his life and reported the incident. After reporting the amusing, yet equally alarming incident, the ashen-faced driver had the car seized whilst investigations were undertaken. The investigation was more on the lines of "well how do we hide this then?" It was decided to blame it on the 'hair trigger' of the gun. The officer concerned was promoted very soon after this and never looked back and rose to the rank of Superintendent. It must have been a case of the file relating to the gun discharge being on the boss' desk when he was looking for someone to promote. For whatever reason his name was at the front of the queue and up the ladder he went. Get in the shit and get promoted.

INTERNATIONAL CRIMINALITY AND BACK TO EARTH

Dennis Williams, a Detective Sergeant with whom I often worked, had a friend who had a printing business in Didsbury. Dennis' 'friends' were usually café, or restaurant owners of Greek Cypriot origin, sprinkled with a few club owners and bar managers and he carried a little black book, which he referred to on a daily basis to see where we would dine for the day and who deserved our non-paying, rent-collecting company. The printer must have done some private printing for him in the past and therefore having been visited thereafter for other little contracts, had Dennis stamped on his memory. He asked Dennis to take a stroll from the police station to his works which was literally just around the corner, as he had something to tell him. It was a sunny day and the distance was only about 400 yards, so we walked and didn't take the car. At this time I was still active with my vehicle repossession sideline for the private detective agency and always had a 'nice ride' such as a Jag, or Ford Granada, for us to swan about in

The story was surprising to say the least. It involved a Nigerian national who had shown the printer some African currency and wished him to print a massive amount for which he would pay many thousands of pounds. The whole enterprise was designed to bring down the Nigerian Government. Hardly believable, but well worth a look as international coups were not an everyday occurrence on the Didsbury division. An offence was inevitable somewhere in it all and, in any case, such a large amount of 'readies', in whatever currency, whether real or not, certainly had an appeal even if we had to go to Nigeria for a holiday if Thomas Cook's currency desk didn't pass them if we tried to change a few.

So with the thoughts of African sunshine firmly in our minds, an appointment was swiftly made for the Nigerian to return to the printers with examples of the currency. Dressed in the obligatory brown printers' coats, stained with ink and a row of BIC biros in the top pocket, Dennis and I were introduced as currency and fine printing experts. We were indeed experts in spending currency and fine dining might have been a fair phrase, but neither of us had printed anything since our schooldays.

With an expert eye, magnifying glasses and rulers we examined the notes for some time. We discussed all the incriminating points, got all the evidence we needed, including the chain in Nigeria. During the lengthy conversation we established that this man seemed to be well connected to a political opposition party in Nigeria and had been assigned to this operation. We couldn't believe the naiveté of the man. How could he trust strangers with what was certainly a capital offence in his homeland? With all the conversation recorded, notes made and banknotes seized for examples he was arrested. We took him back to Didsbury nick, where he remained totally honest and transparent. He expected to be released and did not really believe he had committed any offence as he was in England where he believed anything was possible, at a price. He was probably correct but had just picked the wrong printer.

We reported the circumstances to the Foreign Office via Scotland Yard. It seemed the best idea as we were well out of our depth, usually dealing with the odd nicked car or burglary and suddenly plunged into international forgery rings and Government coups.

And so a couple of real spies from MI5 were dispatched and travelled up from London to interview him. The Yard advised on the charges and they let them run in Manchester. The unfortunate little man continued to remain incredulous as he pleaded guilty and got 10 years. None of us realized or really cared just how serious the offence was. We were later informed that the judge however independent they claimed to be had been instructed at Government level to keep him out of the way for a while. He did better than that; he ordered that on completion of his sentence, he be deported to Nigeria, where, no doubt, he would never be heard of again.

The Law Lords, in their infinite wisdom have decided that the police were wrong to reject the application of a transsexual to join the police. If he/she should ever be a serving officer, one of the many difficulties he will face will be to search both women and men upon arrest. But there is always an excellent blow job to look forward to, perhaps for his companion on nights. From the experiences I have had and witnessed, the fact that the transsexual "came out" is the only difference, considering that policewomen have always shagged other policewomen and policemen. Gay males have shagged all they can and anywhere they can, even fellow officers, for as long as I can remember.

On the lighter, more hetero side of sex, many officers made an art form of seducing the female inhabitants of the city wherever they were located. If that wasn't an option, they might engage in the "peep," the well-known art of watching sex acts in a variety of locations, known in higher educated circles as the voyeuristic arts. I remember a nameless colleague being disturbed. He was fully naked, with an equally naked young lady in his car on the site, which is now Piccadilly Station. The vehicle with him inside was fully concealed and he had even cleared his presence with the security man, telling him he was taking observations with a lady in the car for cover and agreeing with him to stay away.

Peepers with their own rules and their own unbelievable radar respected no such requests and in any case knew that no such act of serious policing, such as lengthy periods of observations ever took place. Colleague and lady friend, with a full head of steam, and well into the act, suddenly realized they were not alone. Colleague was happy to continue, but lady friend was not amused and having unscrewed and separated themselves with some difficulty in such a small car, started to get dressed. Colleague, forced to follow, also dressed. It was only when he undressed at home to retire to bed, with his wife watching, that he realized he was wearing the lady friend's knickers. The knickers were very similar to Marks & Spencer's gent's underwear, but with the artistic addition of lace on the legs and waist of the pink apparel. Wives were much more trusting in those days, and she accepted the explanation of hubby following through after a curry at the Piccadilly Indian, which was common, necessitating the dumping, so to speak, of the original underwear and wearing a replacement pair obtained from the night security at Marks who appeared amused, for what was an unknown reason. Now that I write it down and report it, it seems beyond belief to me. Are wives, like Lady Justice, really that blind?

The most extreme example of peeping actually occurred during my service in the CID at Didsbury in South Manchester. I accompanied a fellow officer who wanted to show me the best peep on the beat, immediately behind the station. This was a residential area of terraced houses with high walls, garages, and rear entries. The best peeps were to be found through bedroom windows. I declined the offer when I realized he was to climb over and then balance upon several walls, sneak through private gateways, over fences and finally balance on a garage roof to gain the perfect vantage point. Obviously, some were much simpler and in certain circumstances the female was fully aware of her audience and got obvious pleasure from the show she was starring in.

Today the police are populated at all levels with officers of similar suspect mentality and very concerning working practices and beliefs. Whatever their deviations, dishonesty or sexual perversions they could all hide in the police in the knowledge that very few were prosecuted to the point of prison. Most were allowed to resign and in many cases were allowed to remain as serving officers. Set a thief to catch a thief comes to mind or indeed, set a perv to catch a perv. Savile, Hillsborough, the Plebgate affair and so many more haunting examples have all proved that there is a police force for the police force and another for Joe Public. There are departments at all levels to house the mixture of police excuses for specialized departments. Lesbian Community Relations and Black Community Relations, usually staffed by black officers which appears to defeat the object and innumerable others, all of which are difficult to be taken seriously in the knowledge of all the ingrained prejudices within the police force. It does not really matter how many ethnics the police recruit and whatever accelerated rank they reach there will remain the ingrained racial prejudice and with it a total lack of respect.

Each division had a crime prevention officer and the main office of this group of ageing stalwarts was situated in our headquarters building. An inspector and a sergeant ran this fine group of men who visited premises which had been burgled throughout the city. Their objective was to explain to the complainants how poor their security measures had been and how to improve them to prevent a future incident. Such improvements usually included an expensive burglar alarm system and luckily they had the contact number for the local representative of an installation firm. The reasons for such a reference was obvious to all except the complainant, who, in paying such a price, was including the CPO's bung. On retirement from the police, Crime Prevention Officers were usually found employment at their favorite suppliers.

Enterprise was there for the taking. One just needed to watch and listen carefully. One needed only the necessary ambition, because the opportunities were everywhere. Enterprise and invention always seemed to find its way to gold. One needed to listen to the right voices above them, or to the side of them and to develop instincts. It also helps to have the right male gear. Brains and balls is an excellent combination. Maybe the police are too close to the bad guy. That in pursuit, in the art of the chase, it becomes an imperative to think like the quarry itself. Being so close, often causes a contamination, an infection of sorts. To defend against this is difficult at best, if not impossible. As I said earlier, everybody was in on it...and then some. We had cops with yachts and mistresses with fine jewellery and then other cops with the odd Rolls Royce, or top of the range Jaguar. Cops with homes that cops can't afford, bought at the price of common and fruitful infractions of the very law they are sworn to uphold. I tasted the goods. It was a taste too sweet not to. Refusal was too difficult to consider. There was no one to turn to, no one to trust, it was a culture so get on with it.

And then again, additional income reaped additional women and as a result the by-product of sex was jolly good too. There were many friendly women visiting the pubs and clubs. The Ritz dance hall was very popular. It served as a venue for the BBC programme "Come Dancing" on regular occasions. It was also the "grab-a-granny" headquarters and has remained so to this day. If you didn't have sex of some form or other in her or your car, you had to be gay or too choosy, which was never the case with serving police officers, especially the married ones. Well to be honest gay could have been an issue but choosy, never. These elderly queens performed the act as if it was their last. I wouldn't be able to explain it then, but there was always a small hint of desperation in their sex. It made the work a bit easier, with the exception of the work it took just to engage at all with them. To a sexually experienced individual such as me, the rewards were immediate and cost effective. An education that by far compensated for the nostril offending perfume and the masses of Boots Talcum Powder in their generous gussets, damp with excitement.

Whilst serving in the Drug Squad before being moved to Didsbury I had cultivated an excellent informant with whom I had a fantastic working relationship which kept all barbiturates off the streets. If they were stolen in burglaries I'd get a call and they were later recovered with search warrants. In addition to keeping the drugs off the streets I kept my man out of prison. He was a violent individual who was often arrested for serious violence. It was my job to see the Stipendiary Magistrate and persuade him to allow him to continue with his information, which kept the drugs off the streets despite suspended prison sentences imposed at other courts where I had no say.

I asked him to mix with the locals in Didsbury, particularly the druggies who committed wanton burglaries to pay for their drug habits. They would burgle at all times of day, often the homes of elderly people, who did not ever realize the need for a burglar alarm. It was all so easy and to make matters worse they would take personal and sentimental items which they would sell to anyone for a few pounds just to secure a deal to get them through the day.

My best friend, who made the job so easy was immediately totally accepted, because he was already well known to the drug-selling and using populace. They in turn also dabbled in crime, sometimes with large ambitions and committed burglaries on the well-heeled properties in Didsbury regularly stealing very expensive items of jewellery, televisions, music centres and the like.

In addition to my superstar, other CID members had informants with drug connections. On one occasion a drug using individual was arrested and brought to the station by a colleague. His whole demeanor reeked of being a hard case, he was uncooperative from the word go. In his pockets he had a great deal of cash, for which he refused to give an explanation. His attitude was 'if you have got the proof, then get me charged.' He also had a few pieces of jewellery of some quality and clearly had been arrested on a selling spree and was not selling it cheaply as was the norm for the usual shithead junkies. His flat was searched and amongst other items of jewellery was an unusual key. Not being as clever as he thought he was, he had left the paperwork for a safe deposit box in the city. He had ripped off the name and address, but the reference number remained. Despite some considerable persuasion, he would not divulge the location of the box. He was punched, kicked, plugged into the mains and generally inflicted with all sorts of persuasive techniques, but he would not budge. Such tactics were deemed necessary to prevent the usual police inquiries and slogging about on foot, bank to bank and the few safety deposit companies, if indeed it was in Manchester in any case.

His flat had been searched by officers without Drug Squad experience. They had never even considered some of the inventive hiding places we knew of and so two of us with a vast knowledge of searching were asked to return to the flat. Our legendary experience even located drugs before specially trained dogs. His flat was searched again, but this time, every inch was turned over with our considerable expertise. A large amount of cash of about £1,000, which was a fortune in the 70s, was found hidden behind a sliding skirting board. This was an ingenious hiding place, but I had seen this type of concealment before on many occasions when learning my Drug Squad trade. Appearing solid, such a skirting board would sound hollow and loose when kicked, actually, very similar to the owner. The cash was treated as everyone expected, by all assembled. There was little point in lodging it at the station as cash had no evidential value and was often easily accounted for. It served a much better purpose in buying carpets, kitchen appliances and the like for the poverty-stricken officers. Further paperwork was discovered relating to a possible safe deposit box location in a more detailed form, but incomplete with more information and real police work necessary to formulate a complete picture.

We already knew this man must be a serious operator and we visited the safe deposit premises like children in a toy shop at Christmas, but the key didn't fit any of the boxes. The manager of the safe deposit company examined the key and thought it was for a safe, not a box, but a safe was never located anywhere during the entire investigation and interviews.

We still had the other receipt and this did refer to a safety deposit box currently in use at the premises. A search warrant was necessary despite the fact that the man was already under arrest and about to be charged with anything to hold him. In such cases it was perfectly within the law to search without a warrant, but we felt a safe deposit box may be different and subject to more binding privacy laws. It was very clear that we were dealing with a serious operator and the need for perfect continuity was vital to keep the books straight and be evidentially sound throughout.

A locksmith drilled the lock and entry was gained. The box was jammed with cash, jewellery and a book written in some kind of code. We sent the book away to some Government code breakers but nothing came of it. Unless they cracked it without telling anyone and then grabbed the ill gotten gains themselves? The jewellery was clearly too valuable to be put against any old crime report as with TICs and must have been identifiable with close sentimental value to a number of people. Accordingly, we took the unusual steps of attempting to find the real owners – not the norm at all. We were dealing with very valuable items and clearly with considerable monetary value. The jewellery was advertised throughout the force on the usual bulletin sheets with photographs and detailed descriptions. We also circulated the document to the adjoining forces serving the good residential areas of Cheshire and Lancashire via the local police stations. The entire jewellery collection was exhibited, on a pre-arranged evening at Didsbury Police Station. Burglary complainants from many areas came to view the recovered items.

We were startled to see how much was actually identified and felt some pride in actually detecting real crime amongst all the petty burglaries, stolen cars and pedal cycles of our day to day work. We later established from officers on other divisions in a boasting competition that we had 'our trousers taken down' by a scam. Bogus complainants from adjoining county forces attended, usually friends of the serving detectives and most of whom arrived toward the end of the viewing and amazingly all of them identified a few expensive items and their detective friends who were able to write off a few crime reports as a result in addition to the inevitable and lucrative share-out.

The prisoner in custody was having nothing. There were no TICs and there would be a full trial. The weight of the circumstantial evidence of the property from many identified burglaries and his total silence was enough with a few necessary and well-planned verbals to fill the gaps despite his refusal to utter a single word. Whatever property was not identified - and it still remained considerable - was held for three months in the station safe, hidden away in the Detective Chief Inspector's office and taken out on occasions to exhibit to occasional complainants who must have been quite surprised at the cross-examining they received to prevent another scam by colleagues from further afield. Having exhausted all identification avenues the remaining items of jewellery were then supposed to be taken to the central police stores to be later disposed of by auction, or to jeweller friends of the store's manager for the usual consideration. This seemed to be a terrible waste and, as Woolworth's sold "exact" copies of the real items, they were changed during the journey to the stores. Should you ever visit a police auction, you will see very few single items of good quality jewellery and probably for this very reason. But I am not sure where they'll get the tat now that Woolworths has gone, though Poundland might be a good starting point.

Some years ago a safe deposit company in London was burgled and all the boxes opened. Of course, it is the nature of a safety deposit box that the contents are not known. Very few people will admit to owning the contents, fearing attention from the taxman or the police. Arrests were made so quickly that it was obvious that an informant had been the key to the entire operation (forgive the pun). A few days had passed to allow for the odd item of jewellery to go astray and so the story goes that at a police ball in The Savoy Hotel in London, the entire group of detectives involved attended with their wives all sporting a selection of the intercepted proceeds.

On the subject of safety deposit boxes, the Midland Bank premises on King Street were offered for sale. In the bank was a large safety deposit box room and many of the boxes had remained unused for many years. They had been hired in the days of bogus names and addresses, accepted without identification and therefore unidentifiable many years later. All the boxes had to be opened under close supervision for obvious reasons by skilled locksmiths and every item logged. The story goes that three firearms, masses of expensive jewellery and cash all with the accumulated value in excess of £10,000,000 and no one to claim it. What a terrible waste. The bank is now a Jamie Oliver Restaurant and the safe deposit box room is now for private dining and a tourist attraction. It is well worth a visit.

On the subject of booty, we were given information about an Arthur Daley character on the division who was receiving decent amounts of stolen property. He had a cash and carry establishment with piles of genuine purchases. Hidden amongst his genuine purchases were piles of stolen items and it was impossible to differentiate between the two types. A search with a warrant proved this and the subject produced a pile of purchase invoices in no particular order. The store was full to the roof and there was not sufficient time to complete a full audit as the pub was beckoning, the hour was late and realistically we just could not be bothered to search amongst all the dust and accumulated rubbish.

We adjourned to a nearby pub, to regroup, lick our wounds and consider the next course of action. The discussions and planning went on for days, whenever we were in a pub. On this particular occasion we were in a very noisy pub with plenty of background noise. One of the lads phoned the store owner from the pub which all the local villains used. He told our devious victim that he had heard two coppers talking to another man, clearly an informant, who supplied a list of stolen property which he was hiding. He suggested he should get it out as the 'coppers' were to get a real search warrant so there could be no problems when they got him bang to rights. We immediately left the pub and sat in the cars watching from a distance. 'Arthur' nearly had a heart attack shifting washing machines, dryers, microwaves and piles of tinned food as the humping of them was not conducive to his portly frame.

In view of the urgency he had no alternative than to complete the exercise alone. He filled a large transit Luton van and probably lost a stone in weight. He jumped into the cab and drove to another store a couple of miles away, equally bulging with stock and one which we were not aware of. Having been entertained to the point of him having a wobbler we appeared and continued with the previous discussion. The cockiness gone, he broke into tears brought on by exhaustion and the thought of losing everything.

A LITTLE ROMANCE, A LITTLE RAVER AND A VISIT FROM THE OTHER SIDE

I thoroughly enjoyed my time at Didsbury. Whilst not whiter than white I drew the line at committing real crime, which involved actual burglaries and the real commission of actual thefts. Everybody had a 'dabble' in something, but most also drew the line on real criminality. The line was invisible of course and difficult to differentiate from dishonesty was the Robin Hood attitude, where there wasn't really a monetary loser with true ownership and this would never be established in any case. A perfect example is a car radio. In the 60s and 70s they were not fitted as part of the car, but as an added extra. Hauls of such radios were often recovered from lock ups and the chances of finding the true owner were negligible. The prisoner had admitted to a pile of TICs, many crime reports were sorted and the detection rate soared. What of the radios? Well they would be auctioned from stores for some nominal price. Such a waste just could not happen and so every poverty-stricken officer's car eventually had a Bang and Olufsen multi music centre, or similar, thumping away on the journey home. Clearly, it sounds criminal but it should once again be made perfectly clear that we were not a rogue element amongst so many dutiful bobbies. Such behavior was a culture and yes whilst serving the public and Her Majesty in taking the initial oath, we were just following a way of life encountered at every stage and practically every day in so many differing forms. As I have always said, the Hillsborough conspiracy had its foundations within such a culture and writing off so many deaths was merely an extension of such day to day thinking and beliefs we all experienced in the 60s and 70s.

For example the Daily Mail in March 2009 featured the following article under the headline................ON DUTY 1,000 POLICE FOUND GUILTY OF CRIMES. The article reveals that more than 1,000 serving police officers remain on duty despite being convicted of criminal offences such as assault, kerb-crawling, GBH, wounding, robbery and perverting the course of justice. There are at least 77 serving officers with convictions for violent offences which in itself proves the acceptance of violence in the performance of their duty (many chapters in my trilogy illustrate this) and 36 with convictions for theft and again seen as everyday life in the police.

Liberal Democrat Chris Huhne, the coalition Government's Secretary of State for Energy and Climate Control, had a brush with the law over his wife Vicky Pryce's driving points and it resulted in jail time all round for their conspiracy to pervert the course of justice. Yet before this Huhne had unearthed some stunning stuff and as such stated that the public cannot accept how a serving police officer can perform his duties effectively and how he could possibly give evidence in a court of law with the risk of being shown to be dishonest with a criminal record. His brief visit to one of Her Majesty's establishments – HMP Leyhill - appears to have taken his eye off that particular ball and no other MP has taken up the cudgel, probably due to all their particular skeletons in so many cupboards.

Incredible figures show that 1,063 officers serving in 46 forces throughout the UK have been found guilty of a variety of offences. Goodness knows what the total is today. Several years later, there now appears to be nothing recorded for public access, which is hardly surprising. Being the Biggest Gang, with no knowledgeable person to answer to and no real terms of reference the police feel they can continue unabated. Politicians and their skeletons in their various cupboards are hardly likely to rock the boat in case their little world becomes the subject of a further investigation, yet again, only to be filed away for future reference.

Violence what violence

It is Friday, May 7th, 2004, and virtually every newspaper in the world is covering Iraq and the treatment of prisoners. The British police have their own stories, but let me make a variation on a theme. We have been treated to a deluge of coverage concerning the mistreatment of prisoners in Iraq and now Afghanistan to the detriment of many honest serving soldiers and even a serving doctor, who was struck off for misleading a military tribunal. Let us not forget the heroic SAS man who took on the establishment through his wife whilst incarcerated for what can only be seen as a petty offence in the world in which he existed. This man has risked his life on so many occasions and yet when it suits, he was totally shit on by the establishment. It appears to have been conveniently forgotten, by an army of do-gooders, that these so-called victims of the British Army are the same people who have been killing both British and American servicemen in innumerable acts of cowardice disguised as religious zeal.

The jailers have seen their colleagues die. The Military Police who interrogate these animals have seen first-hand their colleagues butchered in a police station, having been badly equipped by the Ministry of Defence with minimal ammunition and inadequate fire power.

The images the rest of us see, the ones blasted on the evening news, shaped and edited at a political whim of the studio money. The rhetoric and reports we hear, carefully crafted from writers who are under strict MOD control, nowhere close to the actual carnage, the sights and sounds removed from our distant lives, these things are not images to the soldiers and workers in occupation. They are the reality each of them is faced with. To them the images are all too real, too close and will not easily go away or fade with the soft corruptions of time. Construction workers, torched in their car, their mutilated bodies then dragged about the streets, soldiers killed by the army they are training and other horrific incidents.

These so-called horrific incidents, shown in photographs, some of which were faked, portray prisoners, naked, on a dog lead, tied to a bed with underpants on their head, secured together on a floor or being threatened with a gun. As Lieutenant Michael Drayton, of the American National Guard, commander of the 870th Military Police Company had the balls to say: "You have got to understand. Although it seems harsh, the Iraqis only understand force. If you try and talk to them one to one as a normal person, they won't respect you. So you have to be forceful with them in certain ways." How refreshing, a similar philosophy to that which existed in Wythenshawe during my CID service, with the incestuous scrotes who abounded and thrived until 'disciplined.' There is a frustration factor dealing with the Iraqis. Everybody wants to choke them. And so it is in the UK where hard working British subjects see jobs, homes and masses of money going to the mass of immigrants who offer nothing to this country.

Most of these prisoners have been engaged in terrorist activities. They have caused death of army personnel, as well as Iraqi citizens, including innocent women and children. And what physical treatment did they suffer? They were made to wear a dog lead, their own underpants and, on occasions, they wore each other when they were bundled together and tied. These people behave like animals and are simply being treated in kind. These actions are no different to those performed by the British Army from as far back as anyone can remember, through the Black Hole of Calcutta, two world wars, various smaller campaigns, up to the Falklands and Northern Ireland.

The Daily Mail on Tuesday, May 11th 2004, listed a string of offences allegedly committed by the serving army in Iraq and highlighted in a Red Cross dossier. I thought I was reading from a police manual or Jack Butler's diaries of what were common practices in my early days and even practiced today in lesser degrees. More recently these were commonly used in Northern Ireland by the police and the army. They produced results, they protected the honest public and after all that is the only real point to any of it. They recruited informants and based on that information ambushed and arrested many suspects sometimes shooting the occasional victim to make a point that they were in charge and more importantly they "kept the lid on," though not permanently.

John Stalker intervened in Northern Ireland. In his naïve and confused aim for further promotion it appeared he believed he could actually prove there was a 'shoot to kill' policy in Northern Ireland. He chose to ignore all advice from friends, usually Catholic as he was, not to get involved. Manchester businessman Kevin Taylor at a dinner in Swinton Rugby Club told Stalker, who was sat next to me yet again, that it was suicidal in a career sort of way to accept this position and conduct a full investigation into such practices. He was to leave his own force he knew to be perpetrating the same brand of violence, but without the shootings and complaints of a shoot to kill policy, to such a degree that he could not fail to know about it. The level of such violence inflicted by the police is, of course, always relative to the violence and murders committed by the civilian population. Much more violence was dished out in the ghettos of Wythenshawe than the leafy suburbs of Didsbury where a simple threat would suffice.

Such violent interrogating practices were the rule in Northern Ireland and with Government approval. Stalker who caused so much trouble with his ill-fated investigation was eventually removed, but having done so much damage, things were never the same. His own career came to an abrupt halt as warned by Kevin Taylor, who was eventually to be the unwitting key to his dismissal. The IRA took advantage of the unrest within the police that remained and committed further atrocities in the knowledge that any complaint would be treated seriously, despite the fact they were murdering hard working officers and innocent members of the public.

The mainland police could never match the Northern Irish officers in their expectance of violent reprisals and their actions to defuse such a threat. Of course it remained popular for politicians to criticize the army and their conduct in the knowledge that they could not arrest them as the police could, should they ask too many embarrassing questions. The unbridled violence in the police was wanton and permitted and real comparisons could be made in the treatment of prisoners in the arenas of Iraq and Afghanistan and Wythenshawe and so many areas throughout the UK.

The top 10 accusations aimed at the 'official' behaviour in Iraq and after that Afghanistan are as follows:

1. Beating prisoners whilst hooded, so they didn't know when the next blow was coming.
   This rings a bell.
2. Using handcuffs, fixed so tight and for so long that long term nerve damage was caused.
   Are they not for restraining? Shouldn't injury be regarded as collateral damage?
3. Beatings with pistols and rifles. Slapping, punching, and kicking.
   Substitute truncheon, chair, and desk ruler for pistols and rifles.
4. Pressing prisoners' faces into the ground with boots.
   Substitute Doc Martens because of added comfort for the wearer.
5. Threats of ill-treatment, reprisals against family.
   Mothers were always a good lever to extract a confession especially if stolen property had been discovered in the house and mummy was in danger of arrest.

As I write, two very good friends of mine have been charged with aiding and abetting their fugitive son. There is evidence to suggest that this was done only to force his surrender, in the knowledge that his mother is seriously ill with a complaint that causes blood vessels to burst in her head if excited and under stress. From day one, Cheshire detectives have always been regarded with considerable humour by the surrounding city forces of Liverpool and Manchester. Joking terms such as Gurkhas comes readily to mind. Remember Gurkhas took no prisoners and even today Cheshire police are close to the bottom of the national detection figures, vying seriously with Derbyshire another rural retreat for the less able CID members. Anyway, we digress back to the top 10:

6. Solitary confinement with deprivation of sleep food and water.

   Police cells have always been operated on this principal.

7. Stripping detainees and parading them naked, sometimes hooded.

   This was quite common in my day and more so today with the improvements in forensic examinations, DNA, etc. Suspects are regularly stripped their 'tackle' ridiculed and paraded as the replacement clothing is sought.

8. Exposure to loud music and noise.

   Doesn't this come under the good old sleep deprivation banner? It happened then and probably still does now.

9. Forcing prisoners to remain squatted or standing with arms lifted for prolonged periods of time.

Add kneeling, laid on ground handcuffed, kicked, jumped on and sprayed with tear gas. That gives a fuller police detention procedure of my day, excluding the use of gas a recent addition to the armoury to protect the midgets of the moment, which in my day was substituted with urine.

10. Prolonged exposure of hooded prisoners in the sun for several hours.

    It was only the weather that prevented this one in Manchester. Standing in the rain did not achieve the same result, except in January and February.

    With such an attitude of all is fair game, there were of course few comparatively minor additions to the annual income which were always welcome, but not to be relied upon. I substituted such activities with a little part-time job which grew to such a degree with the additional earnings that it appeared to be my full-time employment with the police as a necessary hobby, pension and all that.

The best laid plans

In my travels and from an introduction already related, from Dennis Williams, I had met a private detective named Chris More and his partners, Frank Whelan and Sid Almond. Their main clients were finance companies who instructed them on a great deal of trace work, specifically on cars that had been acquired on hire purchase. It transpired that the customer had left the address, or of course, never resided there in the first place. Not all deals were fraudulent and many of those who were termed as hirers just failed to make the payments and the car was demanded back by the HP company. The hirers as they were legally referred to were, of course, by that stage, driving for free, they were not paying the HP. They were ducking and diving and often hiding the car to prevent repossession. Sometimes the finance company would have a copy key and sometimes they would not.

In these instances the driver when actually traced and seen to be driving the car had to be tricked from the vehicle, or even threatened with prosecution as it was by this stage taking and driving away without the consent of the owner. Such procedures were rather fraught with a number of dangers. For an everyday repo agent, it was a normal day's work. As a serving police officer the repercussions were magnified to the point where dismissal could be an issue. I was not supposed to have other employment and could not risk being arrested. For this reason I carried only my driving licence, no police warrant card, or anything which would give a clue to my actual occupation. I carried a letter of authority signed by the directors of the company authorizing me to repossess any vehicle for which I carried copies of HP documentation.

I had spent a great deal of time with the directors of Contact Investigations in my police days whilst wining and dining at their expense with Dennis Williams. Dennis is fondly remembered as my supervising Detective Sergeant, an ace blagger and shagger extraordinaire, and a hero in my eyes. The repossessions were not something Dennis wished to be concerned with, he was above that and had his own little regular earners, some of which I had no knowledge of and those I was aware of, but are not suitable for publication.

I took on the responsibilities of the finance company repossessions which at that time were few and far between, but certainly as they arose provided a welcome addition to my police salary. This was an unknown little earner in the CID. We had all visited a non-paying member and repossessed the odd piece of furniture and the occasional car but never to this extreme. Whilst various CID members debt collected for their business 'pals' they had no experience of how to treat a situation such as this. In effect this was a real little business and it was not really what they wanted being what appeared to be too much like hard work when equal sums were available in their little bent worlds for much less effort. Accordingly, I had no competition for this business even from Dennis himself.

Being such an isolated little earner the internal affairs investigation branch was not really tested. The Y department as it was known was fully occupied with various investigations involving esteemed CID members indulging in the usual extracurricular activities of offering protection, collecting debts, selling stolen jewellery and the rest. However, my repo activities were still tantamount to skating on thin ice and I was walking a fine line. The danger was actually in raising the interest of the office snouts who without the bottle to do the same were consumed with jealousy and only had to look out of the office window to see me turning up one day in a Triumph Spitfire and a few days later in a Ford Granada, admittedly somewhat often beaten up due to cabbying, but still in a luxury car bracket compared to the wheels driven by the everyday detective. In addition to the luxury cars I had to come back to reality and drive many Hillman Avengers, the favoured wheels at the time of the Liverpool Pakistani taxi-driving community. Wessex Finance Company was then part of the Hovis Group and appeared to have more money than sense. They would allow garages to sell these Hillman Avengers on the minimum of factual information, no deposit, dubious identification and certainly bogus addresses. The end result was masses of identical cars in Liverpool requiring repossession.

The Chief Inspector with the nickname 'Strange' would sniff about, attempting to solve the mystery of my 'fleet' of cars, which changed weekly, sometimes thrice weekly and which I had explained away as a neighbour with nowhere to park his car dealing stock. Norman, the office clerk and unofficial Radio Didsbury, had an incredible knowledge of all the gossip throughout all the D Division third section that was the leafy village and surrounding area. He kept me fully informed of the levels of suspicion. Being the clerk was as equally exciting as boring and he took great pleasure in my little business with no expectation of any financial return whatsoever. This was his idea of entertainment, he just liked to know it all and any secret was there to be broken and so there was no point in trying to hide anything from him. The suspicion from the snouts and indeed 'Strange' escalated to the degree that I started to park elsewhere in the village only to find 'Strange' attempting to follow me

Being a Detective Chief Inspector of some repute you would have thought that he would think out of the brackets and look at my house in Cheadle Hulme, which always had a selection of repos parked in the drive and if really busy also on my neighbours' drives, awaiting collection with a low loader, sent by the finance company on my next period of days off.

Repossessing these taxis was an art. I had to be devious to the extreme. Whatever you may think of Asians, their laziness and dishonesty, they are very sharp and able to spot a scam a mile off. I was equally crafty and took great pleasure in getting one over on one of the world's tricky bastards. I would choose to ride in the taxi I wished to repo and act as a paying fare looking for an address, rather than follow and risk detection, until the driver got out of the car. Believing that his passenger was a big fare based only on the fact that I was wearing a tie and jacket and not on the way home from court, or the obligatory Liverpool shell suit, the driver in the belief that we were to drive many miles in my search for the address would decide that he would need to fill up and often asked for a £10 note up front. This I gave him, we filled up and as he wandered off to pay at the kiosk, contemplating his jackpot fare I would either use the key he had left in the ignition or my own if he did not. It was a simple matter to jump into the driver's seat and hit the road.

Only a few minutes later, if that, I would hear the radio crackling with the excited Pakistani taxi drivers in the area, plotting the ambush points to take the car back from me and whilst the conversations were in Urdu or whatever, the Liverpool road names were not and I was able to fill in the gaps, avoid any town centre names where they were lying in wait and nip onto the multi-storey at the St George's Hotel, where the cars were stored for a few days thereby negating the need to run the road blocks

Inevitably some repossessions were difficult. Owners would turn up unexpectedly before I had got the car started with the jiggling of the poorly cut key. I wasn't too bothered with the threats of violence as I could restrain and tie up the arms of anybody with wrestling moves without any real injuries. Such altercations would lead to an arrest of yours truly, on a few occasions until the situation had been fully explained, telephone confirmation with the office confirmed and off we go again. More of a brief detention, really, an occupational hazard I suppose. This actually occurred more times than I would wish to remember as every time I was looking the sack from my day job in the eye, but I got to know a couple of officers and I was able to engage them in time honoured Biggest Gang fashion to speed it all along in a much more relaxed atmosphere and without a sit in the cells, but continuing to hide my true employment.

As the number of cars which required repossessing increased, there was never enough time to totally dedicate to finding specific vehicles, where actual foot-slogging was necessary especially when the office could not give me a lead. Often they had established the likely location of a car and were continuing to attempt to find an actual address. Whilst such enquiries were continuing to try to trace the hirer, which was the normal practice and this enabled me to move on to the easier targets.

I would hold a file of the 'stickers' and on a couple of occasions I was happily driving about Liverpool looking for one of my more recent instructions when I would see one of the vehicles I had held on my wanted list for some time. In such circumstances I would not have the paperwork to produce if apprehended, but took the car anyway and would deal with the consequences as they occurred. Of course I didn't have the key either so I had to trick the driver out of the car. Such an eventuality was inconvenient and time consuming, but was generally due to my own incompetence and casual attitude to detail. Had I carried a briefcase, I would have had all the paperwork necessary but I was not prepared to risk it being stolen, being searched when arrested or even found by my DCI 'Strange.'

I would in this situation have to abandon my car and attempt to get the wanted vehicle back to Manchester. Before I could do so on one occasion I was stopped by the boys in blue, because the car had been reported stolen. Who could blame them for not accepting my explanation? I had to sit in the cells for a few hours whilst the paperwork was delivered to the police station, where it was eventually examined. Of course, inevitably, everyone was out to lunch at the finance company and I was forced to sit it out. I couldn't declare my occupation and was soon released when it was all sorted out.

The beauty of this secondary occupation was that I never had to drive my own car. I just had to hang on to the repossession and drive it about until a new one came up. I only chose the Jags, the TR4s, and the Granadas. Turning up at Didsbury nick in a different car never raised an eyebrow initially in an atmosphere where everyone had additional "hobbies" which entailed a little earner. They always expected me to be up to something as I did with them and, indeed, when I left I was presented with a tankard engraved with a wheel and a deal of cards. It would be silly to suggest that I wasn't the only one with an extra even honest sideline.

However, not all sidelines were totally in keeping with the law of the land if viewed in a boring and serious context. In one such instance I had a colleague who was running a couple of prostitutes and living off immoral earnings. This little business had innocently come into being as the officer had visited a burglary, found the female occupants to be very sociable and very soon had the usual sexual extras only to establish later that the little raver was actually on the game. Quite by chance he found her plying her trade in a city hotel. This could have raised fears of 'blackmail,' but no, in reality a new business opportunity where he enjoyed the fruits of the lady and her friend who he later rented out through the concierges at the airport hotels, enjoying the sexual benefits in addition to the added commission calculated as a finder's fee rather than the poncing which it actually was.

I had been married for some years and we were paying the bills with relative ease. I watched colleagues in a similar position as I was struggling with comparable overheads and resorting to any 'little' earner often on the wrong side of the law. It seemed necessary to maintain a stable home life with the rather arduous social life operating like a parallel existence. I had a strange sense of pride in that I didn't have to stretch the definition of the Theft Act too often to make ends meet. All I had to worry about was the internal discipline side which was much more strict than today and would undoubtedly have resulted in dismissal.

Today there are serving police officers as already outlined with criminal records for a variety of serious criminal offences, which include assaults, burglaries and fraud. The number of repossessions per month was growing and with it my stash of readies, some of which I did not declare at home. I had a safe fitted in the wall of a fitted wardrobe, the size of a brick to which there was only one key. I kept the readies for home emergencies and more importantly it provided for the additional social and resulting sex life. Despite so many attempts to break out of this dodgy corner, in a career sense, it remained an honest little earner. I just couldn't find a similar situation to that of my 'poncing' colleague, which ably covered all his requirements in one easy stroke, so to say.

Between all the lockups, the violence, the verbals and the occasional real police work, there was still a great deal of feminine interest. It seemed to grow as I grew in financial confidence. It is true money makes money and with it comes an entirely different lifestyle. It matured in me with rapid evolutionary expedience. Due to the hours I was actually working and the accompanying social life I had to stop my wrestling training.

This was amateur wrestling which required a great level of fitness and if ignored or undertaken on a casual basis could have easily resulted in serious injury. I had commenced with amateur wrestling at a stage in life which was generally regarded as too late unless I proved to be particularly talented, which I was not. It was only dedicated training and the fact I was able to fight at a weight much lower than that associated with my height and reach usually allowed for, which kept me relatively safe but rarely winning actual competitions. To compensate for this I would train for three hours a day and diet. Whilst I ran about six miles a day, skipped for three periods of 15 minutes spaced with three periods of 15 minutes on the punch bag. The remainder of the session would be actual wrestling training. I had to cease with competitive wrestling but continued to train and diet properly. My obvious physique appealed to women particularly older women for whom I had a leaning. I was certainly a handful, in so many ways for these women. From my late teenage years of premature ejaculation I had risen again in so many ways to being regarded as quite an adept lover.

Little love life

It was easy to meet girl students and I was always visiting their flats in Didsbury and Victoria Park. One flat had four student teachers. Two of us visited and knowing we were non-smokers, they baked us cannabis cookies with some of the stock my pal had filtered from the evidence store at the nick. This was usually taken from frightened students, who were terrified with the threats of life imprisonment for drug possession. My colleague being a father regarded it as a public duty to put the fear of imprisonment into the student types. One such night my car was stolen from outside the student's flat. Embarrassingly I phoned to report the theft. The car was a black Mini with a 1275 MG engine and twin carburettors. I could hear a chase on the station radio over the telephone. It was my car. I could hear the pursuers remarking on the speed of the vehicle, which eventually stopped. The thieves ran away and made good their escape

One of them must have been a DJ because he had left two carry boxes of records. The car was intact. I went to Longsight Police Station to collect it and, in doing so, called in the CID office to fabricate a reason to be on the division in case the question was asked. When the resident detectives weren't hanging prisoners from windows in a confessional moment, they were setting each other alight with a series of well-planned practical jokes. The offices were situated on the first floor and faced onto the large yard where, in my learned cadet days, I actually did drill training. At night it was deserted, but during these hours it was often the practice of the Life On Mars brigade to hang reluctant prisoners, who were not co-operating in admitting their offences from an open window by the ankles. On one occasion a detective lost his grip and dropped such an individual who luckily was saved by a large pile of coke, stored in readiness to stoke the boilers for the building's heating system.

As I continued with such an arduous love life I was of course getting older and the option of chasing more mature women diminished. This was due simply to the fact that despite the age difference remaining the same we were all getting older and had I continued with 'wooing' them, I would have had to iron them first. I had to change my outlook on my sexual requirements and tried to pull the younger models which populated Didsbury in abundance. My older heart was not really in it, I found the younger end somewhat dense and lacking in many qualities that age matured. They fell in love too easily, were never off the phone and could become quite embarrassing. I had known of colleagues arriving home to find the 'young girlfriend' sat on the garden wall. I suppose this somewhat chauvinist attitude was easily reflected in my lacklustre chatting up. As a result I did not then, have the successes I had enjoyed over the years because I tended to dispense with the romantic nonsense and immediately make it clear that I was married and only wanted a sexual diversion.

Clearly, a few disappointed romantics fell by the wayside with the imagined flowers and chocolates, but this was merely a minor hitch in my sexual exploits soon to be stabilized in chatting up married but younger women, who like me, only wanted real sex without too much romance. However, being totally irresistible as I honestly believed whatever the truth, there was the occasional hiccup when one or two of the married variety decided that they would leave home and we would run away together to pursue love's dream elsewhere. Life's full of disappointments, so they'd be disappointed and I'd be off to 'sexual pastures new.'

With a number of similarly romantically-inclined colleagues we hired a flat from Malcolm Robinson at his first rental venture Brighta Flats. Malcolm over the years became a multi-millionaire and operates nowadays as Wren Properties.

Malcolm is a small cherubic individual with an eye for profit at every turn. In his younger and informative years he became the subject of police attention by attempting to draw his legitimate rent from a reluctant tenant. Despite his cherubic appearance and stature he threw the cooker of the flat out of the first floor window, threatening to have the tenant follow in a similar manner. I was very impressed. This little incident did not impress those on the local police division and they actually arrested him.

The flat was hired, purely for sex. In good faith I kept the diary and collected the rent. I arranged for the bedding to be changed regularly and the flat cleaned. Despite this, some of my colleagues didn't pay their share, continued to use the flat on the promise of rent on pay day. They left blood and semen stains on the bedding and made no attempt to keep the place tidy. Whenever they were between victims they thought they should not pay their rental instalment. I couldn't do with such childish pettiness and I gave the flat back to the landlords.

Married ladies on the section were everywhere, but nervous at home. They also found it difficult to explain to the unsuspecting husband if he arrived home unexpectedly, the fact that the kindly detective was still continuing with the detection of an old burglary 12 months later. In a state of disheveled hair and wearing the minimum of hurriedly assembled clothing it was bound to be difficult for the most gullible of husbands arriving home early to accept such a feeble explanation. In all my years at Didsbury, such a situation never occurred for yours truly, but I have heard of some hair-raising experiences for others.

Only on one occasion did I experience the panic of the key in the door and was then forced to jump from a bedroom window, wearing only my shoes and clutching a bundle of clothes. After this rather unseemly incident, which could have required an explanation if I had broken a leg or been caught, I attended a burglary at the Montana Hotel in West Didsbury. Very quickly I made friends with the manager, Norman, who happily rented me the basement luxury flat for £20, about three times a week. It was a good earner for him and was paid easily by my ever growing stash of hidden readies. I had the room for only a couple of hours during the early afternoon and so it made no difference to his declared occupancy for the management.

There were never enough police vehicles for the normal divisional use. The entire division had only two Morris Marinas for all the CID officers who were expected to visit all the thefts and burglaries. It was a waste of time trying to get one, so the detective's own car was used and the petrol claimed back. On one occasion I was told to attend at headquarters to see pipe-smoking Superintendent Harold Malone and a solicitor who was complaining about something concerning dubious actions on my part. There were so many I could not possibly recall the reason for this particular summons. As the solicitor knew Malone socially, he was getting personal treatment. Malone knew me well, he had claimed to have detected a murder which was actually solved by me with other Drug Squad colleagues.

I forgot the appointment until the clerk at the Didsbury office phoned me about five minutes before the appointed time, as a reminder. I had to travel the distance of about 10 miles and so I told him to tell Malone I had broken down and stress the fact I was driving my own car in the absence of being properly equipped with a police car. I was in between repossessions and was driving my own souped-up Mini. This looked like a real wreck with a badly fitting fibreglass bonnet hiding an MG 1275 engine from the larger Morris range above the Minis. It was not the safest car as parts of the chassis on each side had to be cut away to accommodate the larger unit.

The clerk laughed and said he would empty my desk into a box as he doubted I would be seen again. I didn't rush, I completed the job I was on and then trundled to headquarters in my Mini. Parking was always an issue and to save time I parked in the yard of Police Headquarters, reserved for Superintendents and above and went upstairs to Malone's office. He clearly thought his word was gospel and was beside himself that his friend had seen him embarrassed by a no show and had to leave for another appointment. Into the office I went and he instantly recognized me from the Drug Squad death despite the fact that I no longer had the long hair and beard.

I had sorted this 'murder' out for him with my trusty informant, a situation he unfortunately didn't recognize in those terms. He also disliked my regular presence in the George and Dragon pub on Bridge Street in Manchester where he was clearly being entertained by the media's finest crime reporters in payment for favouritism in the form of photographs of the accused in big cases. What is today seen as a heinous crime worthy of limitless funds in financing the investigation was an everyday occurrence between the CID hierarchy and media stalwarts and even involved the troops on occasions. I stood with my hands behind my back. Malone was frothing at the mouth. He was a constant pipe-smoker and as a consequence his bottom lip always looked wet and limp and which in his hysterical outburst was now flapping about uncontrollably. His pal's complaint that I had fabricated evidence against a client and, having done so, kicked him around the CID office until he made an admission statement was a load of bollocks and totally groundless, not because of the plausible facts, but because he had no witnesses.

I proved it by getting Malone to phone Detective Inspector Eric Jones, who had taken over from John Thorburn. Eric Jones treated Malone like the buffoon he was and confirmed my explanation, despite the fact he knew little of the detail other than it sounded uncannily like my style of detection, a point he did not relate to Malone. Not to worry. Malone, the "great detective," had an ace up his sleeve.

"What was wrong with your car?"

I explained the earth had come loose and I had to move it about to make contact." This, of course, was a fault with Minis, my 'other' car when I wasn't posing in a repo. It was all I could think of. He was fidgeting with excitement and looking in the area of my concealed hands. Before he could say anything, my hands were facing him, with a sort of Na Na Na Na…Na gesture, covered in oil and grease, which I had smeared on my hands before entering the office. However, I may have had a small problem if he had asked to see the car as it was parked in a bay, next to his in a reserved area, falling apart and looking a heap which it deceptively was not provided the chassis held together. It was a good job I hadn't turned up in a Granada repo bigger, better and newer than his and the excuse would have taken some explaining, as on these cars the earth was actually bolted to the battery and not reliant on a loose screw in the top. Fortunately he was not at all aware of my little hobby, breaking the number one detective rule of taking nothing for granted in an investigation which, of course, he was prone to do and readily proved on so many all too regular occasions.

It was now three nil in the Malone wars, including the 'made up murder' in the Drug Squad. By the time I got back to Didsbury, Eric Jones had stopped my transfer to some 'Siberian' uniformed outpost elsewhere in the city, which Malone had tried to instigate continuing to fester about my conduct and winning ways over which he realized he had little control other than a bullying gesture. Malone did not appreciate that hard-working detectives were the backbone of the CID and a divisional inspector would move heaven and earth to have such men and keep them. They were all, including myself, a breed apart and certainly had various mental difficulties, or should I say deficiencies, especially when compared to the childish views of Malone.

Such an incident was a typical example of the incompetent non-existent supervision, so ably demonstrated by Malone and on so many occasions previously. Malone was not alone, but certainly of a generation who knew better than the new breed of supervisory ranks all exhibiting childish decisions and similar thinking. Such a breed was like a disease creeping into the structure of many working police forces and the hounding of real policemen purely as a naive exhibition of authority was certainly becoming the norm. Such behaviour by an experienced albeit incompetent officer of the old school was unusual, especially because of the existing culture that allowed all kinds of real criminal acts in the pursuit of detection and justice, which as ever involved the liberal use of verbals, the Enid Blytons and the addition of forensic evidence. Then there was the holding of 'court' with journalists and a little drawing of 'rent' in its various forms, which by today's standards is an incredible breach of the ethics expected of someone in public office, but then was just another excuse for a few free pints.

However, the wonderful police vehicles of the day which we used to 'pillage and rape' under the guise of visiting crime scenes, around our section often proved interesting and a serious diversion from the drinking, eating and shagging. We had a Mark III Ford Cortina for a short time which broke up the humdrum of breaching the "Rules of Guidance" in general police work. The vehicle will be remembered by those of a similar age as being the Cortina with the high backed seats. This particular car was maroon and had a special three litre engine fitted and wider wheels and tyres. The suspension was lowered and it went like "shit off a hot shovel." It was fitted with a pop up POLICE STOP sign on the rear parcel shelf. This piece of technical wizardry was operated by a wire, with a ring on the end, which when pulled, stood up. The wire ran from the rear window to the front door post and was mounted on the outside of the internal body work for all to see. The vehicle was fitted with a loud siren and a magnetized blue light, which we could stick on the roof, like Kojak, the bald-headed, lollipop-sucking New York detective of 70s TV played by the late great Telly Savalas, who sadly died on January 22nd 1994 just a day after his 72nd birthday.

I can't describe what a great feeling it was to blaze through the busy streets with light flashing and siren sounding often to only catch last orders at a local hostelry, or the act at the Golden Garter.

One afternoon a bank robbery alarm was activated in the Withington area in the South of Manchester. The central control room put out a general emergency call as was standard practice to any cars in the area. We were a mile away, we had a siren and blue light and I was driving. What more could we need for a hare-brained drive through midday traffic with total authority to do so? We were halfway down Kingsway, an arterial road to the South of Manchester. Tommy Giblin was cowering in the front footwell, pleading for me to stop, afraid to look out of the car window. I was eventually grounded from driving this particular car and, indeed, anything else with more cc than a Marina. Again as a result of the namby-pamby leadership creeping in and yet another weak decision giving no consideration for the fact that I was attempting real police work, albeit in my own fashion.

Just by chance on another day I had got behind a car which was being driven erratically with four scrotes clearly having a ball inside. It was worth a stop and look, but took off at great speed as I sounded the siren and signalled it to stop. The chase went on for a while with my colleague updating control on the radio of the vehicle's speed and direction. Eventually we drove into Wythenshawe, tyres screaming, siren blaring and the traffic ahead hugging the curbside to avoid the lunatic in front of me.

In an attempt to make Wythenshawe habitable and a little more pleasing to the eye, distracting from the row upon row of identical red brick local authority houses, the council had built wide grass verges in front of the houses, often going back from the road for up to 80 yards. Safety was becoming an issue and rather than risk anybody being hit with the car ahead, verging on the boundaries of out of control I decided to push the car off the road. In true Starsky and Hutch style (another popular 70s TV programme), I saw an uninhabited area and planned my manoeuvre as I drew alongside. The idiots in the car were all waving and gesticulating, never considering what was to come next. As I drew alongside I threw the wheel over and collided with the moron's vehicle shocking him into leaving the road across one of the enormous grass verges. I continued to push at his car until he eventually ran out of any space and drove through a privet hedge into someone's front garden. Despite the number of TICs the scrote had after months of similar car-taking it still did not really compensate in the eyes of the bosses for the damage to both cars and the unfortunate pensioner's garden. So there I was, once again the victim of defeatist thinking and restricted to using my own luxury repossessions, which whilst not exactly driving purgatory, a principle was involved.

We were in Didsbury Police Station when we got a call that the office WPC required urgent assistance at a house nearby. We ran from the nick and piled into the office Marina. My three colleagues had barely got into the car and with the doors still open I pulled away from the kerbside immediately into the heavy traffic, across to the other side of the road and raced, down the outside of the stationary traffic, before turning left in front of them all onto an open road at a traffic signal controlled junction.

Calls to police officers requiring assistance always brought out the Biggest Gang element in all of us and all was done to assist whatever the consequences. We soon arrived and equally, the individual causing the distress just as quickly realized that such behaviour was not a career move more a defining moment in his sad little existence. Realization was immediate, at the moment he met our office's answer to Hannibal Lecter. This character (and thank God he was one of us) would throw his victim to the floor, pin him face down and slaver all over the side of his face and neck. He would then whisper "advice" as to the prisoner's conduct and the unbelievable assumption that he had rights. He was bent so low and close to the prisoners ear that the advice was barely audible. This was the ear which usually and inevitably found its way between his lips and in no time his mouth appeared to be bleeding as he looked up from the screaming unfortunate writhing on the floor to his gasping colleagues with a strange smile and glazed eyes. This was certainly extreme by any standards, perhaps entertaining, but never understandable compounded by the fact that the victims never complained of the assault and the resulting police assault charge to account for the injuries. It may have had something to do with the whispered promise that he had also promised to bite off their balls if they didn't cooperate.

Clearly by now, the content I am writing is causing concern amongst the faint-hearted. To reiterate, such behaviour was an ingrained culture and whilst extreme in some demented cases, it was certainly not a rogue element. Consider the following factual examples.

- A Sussex-based Sergeant was convicted twice of assault and reinstated.
- An officer in Warwickshire was convicted of driving offences, dismissed and then reinstated, but was later under investigation for perverting the course of justice.
- An officer was convicted of kerb-crawling. Not dismissed.
- Five officers all convicted of perverting the course of justice in separate forces were not dismissed in a display of the fact that they were probably disciplined for getting caught rather than committing the act.
- An officer in Leicestershire was convicted of selling forged DVDs, but not dismissed. At his nick, clearly they had no other source for the feature films of the day and so he had to stay so that the boss' Saturdays continued with a takeaway, blagged of course and a nice film.
- An officer in Essex was convicted of a robbery and not dismissed. Whatever the actual circumstances, it had to be serious for him to be charged in the first place, but then to remain in the force is amazing. How bad can it get?
- Three officers in Cambridge were convicted of assault, but continued on duty to wreak further violence and havoc on the unsuspecting public and were certainly not dismissed.
- An officer in North Wales was convicted of forgery, but again not dismissed.

All the above are relatively recent matters and concern forces throughout Britain again giving credence to the assertion that this is a definite culture and keeping the long-standing traditions of the Biggest Gang alive and well.

Obviously, just from these few examples there is proof of a defined culture in the police where a rooted belief that nothing will come of any detected criminal behaviour as they believe they are answerable to nobody. As with the Hillsborough conspiracy and the Plebgate affair serving police officers believe that they can write and do anything without any fear of the consequences whatsoever.

With such revelations can the following circumstances and newspaper headline be such a surprise....CAUGHT ON CAMERA, A COP SHOPLIFTING AT ASDA.

A Manchester WPC Kate Ward was filmed on CCTV removing tags from clothing and was apprehended by security staff. She hid the clothes under other shopping which had already been paid for. This was clearly a premeditated act of theft and yet the woman, a serving police officer was only cautioned. She has resigned with no criminal record. How can such a punishment reign alongside other such offences being prosecuted by the police generally and taken to a full court hearing even in the case of struggling pensioners etc. Again the Biggest Gang in Britain, totally out of control, with no one to answer to and still protecting their own whatever the circumstances.

Detective Chief Inspector Eric Jones was a real detective, capable of anything, but with the rough edges exhibited by many of us, trimmed off. He honestly tried to serve the public good with only a few deviations from the actual codes of practice. He was totally different to John Thorburn. He had the same love of TICs and tidy paperwork, but loved a good joke. Remember, I had seen him setting fire to a colleague in the toilet at Longsight. His Detective Inspector had ablutions like clockwork and every morning he would disappear into the toilet block with his daily paper. Trousers around his ankles and elbows resting on his knees allowing the paper to be spread its entire width. Eric made a torch from the previous day's read, lit it with a lighter and when ablaze just threw it over onto the paper, which was quite soon equally ablaze, as the DI hurtled from the cubicle in his underwear and shirt tails attempting to extinguish the blazing papers.

We had a typist, grossly overweight and unpopular with Eric as he was a health and fitness freak. It was the first time I had heard of the clingfilm over the toilet ruse. With this typist it was a particularly effective practical joke. Being the size of a horse she peed like one and it could be heard on a normal occasion from the corridor when passing the toilet. Eric was from the school which felt women should pee and fart quietly if indeed they had to. The screams were heard throughout the building and a uniform sergeant even came up from the floor below to check that an 'interview' had not got out of control and that the preservation of a murder scene was not necessary. I can only imagine the trajectory of the pee as her urine hit the clingfilm.

This poor lady was the victim of other milder practical jokes, such as turning back the clock in her office, putting cold water in her flask of hot coffee, leaving invisible Jensen violet dust on her envelopes to dye her fingers with an irremovable purple dye – a series of wizard japes. This dust was used in the field to catch thieves in the workplace, where the substance was put on money in the locker room and which could be easily seen in an instant as it reacted to the moisture on hands. Being of a permanently sweaty state the typist was a perfect subject and the dye spread effectively all over her 'chubby' little hands. The clingfilm incident was undoubtedly the last straw, she grabbed her coat and handbag and was never seen again.

Many such stories of Eric were common place. He was an avid weightlifter and bodybuilder in his younger days and later took up long distance running, losing a considerable amount of weight with it. I later found out that he had a strange medical condition which was never fully diagnosed. He ran so much to keep his weight down because, when he passed a certain weight, he was prone to black outs which oddly did not occur below 12 stones.

He loved the use of the English language. He also loved the sound of his own voice. When he left the police, he became an after dinner speaker of some repute. His attention to detail came to the fore with his attention to all the necessary detail in the crime reports. He was a real detective, promoted through the ranks and knew all the strokes. He spent a great deal of time reading crime reports in detail, even telephoning the clients to confirm they had actually had the endorsed visits which in itself was a little 'shitty' and disconcerting, especially as a small percentage avoided a physical visit which coincided with the Royal Oak opening hours. Eric was well aware of this and always a step ahead.

Having submitted such reports for completion and signing off it was never a surprise to get them back via the office clerk with a perfectly handwritten note carefully scribed by Eric, taking full advantage of unknown words especially at O level, but indeed the Queen's English in the form of a to do list and a bollocking. He was not a great fan of drinking due to his weight issues and as a result would object to our six o'clock cocktail habit in the Royal Oak. As 6pm approached he would sometimes quite childishly order us to tidy up the comments on the crime reports. I suppose such actions were good for discipline as I look back and the output of the office certainly improved if only with tidy crime reports. In the bosses' eyes at headquarters such apparent supervision certainly proved he was supervising properly and that we were playing at what was after all the game.

We would write replies with the reasons why we had not taken the action he suggested and so on, until one was proved wrong. With Eric's grasp of CID work and his writing abilities, with his expensive fountain pen, in such a flowing style, it was a one sided competition. This was, however, only a paper exercise where nobody really and honestly expected a crime to be detected by pure detective work. There just was not the time.

On one occasion he examined a crime report with which I had gone through the motions, ticked most of the boxes and whilst it was not detected that wasn't really the object of the exercise. It was nice and tidy and fit for filing. In this instance the Chinese complainants had returned home and found a man in their house, in the early stages of searching the bedroom drawers. They were face to face for a second before he ran out of the house. Of course this was the simpler times of the 70s. They were not tied up, beaten or raped as is popular today and in fact no property was missing as they must have caught him in the act before he could find anything worth taking. They reported the burglary with a 999 call, an officer attended and actually drove around the area looking for a man with clothing as described.

Strangely many of the shitheads committing burglaries believed that once they had left the house they were invisible and were often found wandering the streets, totally oblivious to anyone else. I visited the house the following morning as it was in the log as a crime follow up allocated on that day. It was a simple break in, a window had been forced and the house was not alarmed. The good old reliable Fingerprint Department visited, threw white powder everywhere, never found a print and duly left. There was nothing else to do. I wrote the report up as undetected with no further action left to be taken and to be filed. Such matters were dusted off when a few TICs were in the wind and seeking allocation. Eric came back with his usual prose which basically boiled down to: "When did you show them mug shots at the Criminal Records Office?"

Where there was a witness to any offence it was a public relations practice to transport them, usually during an evening, to Longsight where the Criminal Records were based. This was usually inconvenient, time-consuming and actually fraught with danger as there was always the likelihood that a miscreant could be screaming and hanging from a window in the CID office also at Longsight, but at the other end of the long building. I replied with: "I had mentioned such a visit but they said, we all look the same to them," which I thought would touch his sense of humour. It did. He signed off the crime, but never let other endless comments rest or go away for months and for this one highly amusing, winning comment I was destined to endless writing on crime reports in relation to equally pointless non-events.

A better class of recruit

One of the detectives based at Didsbury Chris Barnes was a 'proper chap,' a very well-spoken individual with an apparent public school education. He had an enormous plum in his mouth. I had worked with him in the Drug Squad where we had many entertaining evenings using his well turned-out appearance and his amazing elocution to great effect. We would pretend that he was distant Royalty and that I was his police bodyguard and with this little ruse we had great success. However, his 'Royal' accent actually got me into a tremendous fight in a Manchester nightclub. We were stood at the first floor bar near to a couple of stocky smartly-dressed drunken scrotes, who wanted to take the piss out of his Prince Charles accent. The situation deteriorated to the point where the more aggressive of the two was asking Barnes to come outside and fight. He could not take or have an answer to the educated piss-taking emanating from Barnes any longer as he was completely humiliated with every reply to his aggressive comments.

I decided to step in, Barnes was not a fighter and this lad looked handy and clearly had confidence in his own abilities. His face and head through his short cropped hair were scarred with what were the marks of several fights, perhaps on the plus side not winning ones. Obviously though he was game to have a go, but maybe not as expert as he believed. I was still able to have a real go, with my wrestling training still ingrained in me. Unlike body-building and circuit-training such a depth of fitness remains in the psyche and remains above the average man in the street in ability and agility for many years.

This was not an average man; he was stocky and confident and could certainly fight. I did not wish to reveal we were police as we were off our division and questions could be asked, so decided to get on with it. The hard case relished the challenge and made for the stairs with me following. As he trod on the first step to descend the staircase I decided on discretion being the better part of valour and I kicked him hard on the back of his head sending him spiralling down the stairs. But he was surprisingly well balanced and was able to prevent himself falling and broke the likelihood of a headlong collision with the wall by catching the hand rail. No mean feat and he was evidently much more agile than I had given him credit for. He was in the laboured process of pulling himself upright and was clearly rather annoyed, to say the least. Again I decided discretion was yet again the better part of valour and ran down the stairs as he was clearing his head and kicked him again in the chest. He didn't fall this time so I gripped his head at the cheeks and then by the ears and butted him as I followed up with the benefits of numerous hours of bag work. I rained blows to the head in the region of his jaw and mouth, attempting a knock out but failing miserably.

This time he did however fall down the remaining stairs and on piling in a heap at the foot of them, I was back on him, stamping on his head and bending to punch him. As I did so I was pulled off him and punched heavily by my unseen assailant. Another joined in and they were both trying to punch and grab me. I never noticed they were doormen and gave back what I could as the blows rained down on me.

The owner Mike Sullivan appeared: "Stop, stop it's a copper, you are belting a copper, oh fucking hell this is a real problem." By then I was bleeding from the nose which often bled having broken it five times previously in rugby and wrestling. It looked much worse than it was. That's more than could be said for my adversary, he was covered in bruises on his face and bleeding profusely from his mouth. In the melee on the stairs and the fight at the bottom I had somehow ripped his bottom lip in the inside of his mouth down to his chin. When he tried to talk, it flapped about in a very strange way and had clearly come well adrift. The bouncers panicked and immediately left the club and were never seen again. This was of course unnecessary, it was an honest mistake and the club owner was a pal. It was agreed that Mike and his wife would be witnesses at court, they had seen the tail end of the fight and with a script we all agreed it all went to plan and there we go again, onwards and upwards back into our unrelenting duty to the Queen.

Chris Barnes' wife had very wealthy parents and, whilst he admitted to being uneducated despite the best efforts of his family, he enjoyed all the trappings of wealth. When the Barnes' decided to refurbish their home, they did so with a vengeance. The end result was that in his absence, whilst on holiday Eric Jones' office was carpeted with the best unworn Wilton, cut and fitted to size having been expertly removed from Barnes Towers. In addition, a few smaller pieces of occasional furniture came along with a coordinated set of curtains and pelmet. This was certainly a home from home and Eric was over the moon with his refurbished office. Other senior officers visited from all over the city having heard of Eric's fully furnished and carpeted office. They had called in to inspect the room as though his office was a stately home. The carpet wasn't too bad on the knees either, it was 100% wool and easy on the backside of any young lady, having nowhere else to go in the middle of the night.

The boss Eric was above all a fair man with his own set of values and certain things in life took priority. My wife had just had our first child, a daughter, who was constantly being sick after feeding. The family GP assured us that it was normal and prescribed some sort of mixture with seaweed as the base. This didn't work and we took her again to the GP and I insisted in no uncertain terms that we be sent to the Duchess of York Hospital for babies in Burnage, which is now a block of flats.

On arrival, she was immediately fed with some urgency and on cue she was sick with projectile vomiting which certainly focused the prognosis. She was immediately admitted, put on a couple of drips and we were told she was within hours of dying of malnutrition and could still only be regarded as 50-50. This was all down to the useless GP who I later gripped and left in no doubt that he had come very close to being a permanent resident of Stepping Hill Hospital. A few months later he gave up General Practice and went to work in the casualty department of a Stockport hospital.

The point I am making is that Eric immediately told me to take as much leave as I liked to keep my wife company at such a dreadful time. There was no question of days in lieu against my holidays, he just covered my absence for four days. My daughter quickly improved after she had been operated on and a valve in her stomach had been repaired. He was a decent man and we all worked for him – when we weren't in the pub or shagging that is.

The obvious choice for a romantic interlude when on nights was the office car, although this was not the most romantic location as at this time it was a beige Morris Marina. Nights were the only time any of us on the 3rd section could actually get to use the car. Inevitably there were a few tight bastards who regarded the office car as their own property and passed it amongst themselves. These were generally off the 4th section, where on several occasions their personal vehicles had been vandalized by Wythenshawe scrotes. Because of such occurrences we did not protest too strongly, we just wanted them to know we were not stupid. It was also always believed that the men on the Wythenshawe area should have priority as they had a bigger patch. One of the principals of this school of thought was Joe Carter, who was obsessed with the car, even to the point of fabricating the need for it. I was to see

Mr Carter, much later in life, when out of the police and actively engaged in building my private detective agency.

I was conducting personal injury claims investigations on behalf of insurance companies. At this time Manchester Police was insured by Zurich Insurance. Joe made a claim for disability. It was a common and very popular practice to fabricate accidents whist on duty and submit an insurance claim with the intention of being 'returned unfit' for police work. Such a situation had a real appeal because being returned unfit meant that the value of the compensation and resulting pension was greatly increased. Many officers making such claims inevitably had another source of income, usually a business which was becoming so successful that being in the police was an encumbrance. I knew the feeling well, but strangely when I decided to retire I did so without any such claim. To this day I can't understand why, it was an immediate very worthwhile earner and I must have been having a brainstorm. Claiming to have an accident meant that the 'injured party,' left with a lump sum and a pension for life and I had certainly missed out. In claiming for his suspicious accident Joe Carter forgot to mention he had a painting and decorating business and ladies' hairdressers with a suspicion of a third enterprise. He became a star of one of my early videos and I suppose the financial loss was considerable. They say, 'the wheel always turns' and for Joe my memories of struggling without a police car quickly persuaded me that a nice little invoice to the insurers was certainly better than any unfounded loyalties I had for him.

I owed nothing to anyone. I was always my own man and something like this caused me no strain of conscience whatsoever. I had left the police because I felt I had been let down, I fought my way to success and in doing so my personal life suffered.

When performing my detective duties I actually preferred to drive around in a Ford Granada Ghia visiting scenes of crime, the little victims and meeting the Fingerprint Department. My vehicle of course was a finance company repossession in any case, but on occasions I didn't have any choice and the office car might have been helpful. I could not keep the cars indefinitely and had to return them to the hire purchase company eventually. One night, I was driving a TR4 and whilst it was excellent for pulling the students the vehicle was hardly practical for scrambling lust. Bucket seats and gear levers are not what an amorous rumble is all about. There was no back seat. The office Morris Marina was the obvious choice, despite the only thing it had going for it was a back seat and its own lock up garage off the beaten track at a local car showroom. Being on a main road, Didsbury Police Station rented several private garages on land owned by the car showroom. The garage could also be closed from the inside, ensuring total privacy. Didsbury had a professional peeper and without doubt I would have been fair game had I attempted my amorous liaison anywhere without four walls and a door. The car itself was used 24 hours a day and very rarely valeted unless Inspector Eric Jones saw the inside and had to wade through the empty bottles and chip papers. His innate tidiness did not stop at crime reports and he was in his element with the office car. To summarize, it was filthy, inside and out, but such things were not considered when a trembler was on offer, especially when there was no struggle with clothing which could all be removed by both parties, without the fear of the inevitable peeper, due to the car being totally concealed in the garage.

Sitting upright with the little raver straddled over me soon raised a sweat due to a mixture of our energetic lovemaking and the less than romantic plastic seat coverings. The sweat, running like a tap, down my back, then loosened the dirt on the seat, which was then smeared on my back from the waist up to an area around my shoulder blades. This horrible residue only became apparent when I was undressing in daylight, in front of my wife as I returned from the night 'duty' I had just completed and as she was up and about, getting ready to leave for work. We often crossed paths as I was returning home and she was leaving for work in a bank in the city centre. I still trained to a degree but not to the YMCA standards and the explanation of my stripping to do bench presses on a dirty bench in the station cellar with training weights was readily accepted.

The alternative didsbury populace

During the 70s the population of Didsbury consisted of many middle-aged, law-abiding citizens, who still had a lot of faith in the police and were often phoning with information which they picked up on their travels or by peeping through the net curtains. They were all frustrated Miss Marples and were encouraged to do so, if only for the odd personal visit for tea and freshly-baked scones. One such call concerned a well-known Didsbury family, the Bullers.

The infamous Bullers were petty villains, but always trying to break into the big time. They were a strange mix of half-caste Caribbean and gypsy travellers - rhythmic hard men, so to speak. The call stated that they were breaking up metal bars in their rear garden, which was enclosed by a tall wooden fence. Scrap metal was always seen as yet another 'little earner' and to hear of it being pre-prepared by the Bullers had a certain appeal. Three of us attended in the Marina, which for some strange reason was parked outside the nick. We walked from the front along the side of the house into the rear garden. The house was an old semi on a nice little cul-de-sac with a typical back garden, which in the Bullers' case was a dumping ground for washing machines, mattresses and fridges.

There we saw Sylvia Buller, the infamous mother, with an awesome reputation for fighting and winning and this was usually with men. Also with her was Hughie her son, aged about 16, with two men of obvious gypsy traveller appearance. We could see the metal piled to a height of three feet and of a volume which would have nearly filled a standard transit van. The metal was bronze and we later discovered it was metal stripping used to separate floor tiling on large commercial contracts. There was a considerable quantity and it was clearly of some real value. With the high worth of such scrap metal, it was in the 'top 10' of easier CID earners. That was until we had to prise it away from the Bullers and that's when 'easy' was far from the correct description. As soon as we entered the garden the two men ran off towards the perimeter fence. I went to chase one of them, but was immediately held back with some strength by the lovely Sylvia who grabbed my arm in a vice like grip. Perhaps not the most sensible of reactions and without any consideration for her sex and more for my own preservation in full knowledge of her reputation I instinctively butted her in the face to force her to let me go. Not my best considered move, but totally a reflex reaction. One of the boys had my other arm, but immediately let go, perhaps from shock. Nobody raised their voice to mother let alone butted her in the face. As I mentioned earlier, Sylvia's strength and capabilities were legendary and had to be seen and experienced to be believed. Such a violent act, especially when directed at a woman should, therefore, not be judged too harshly.

One of the men was caught by the legs by one of the other officers as he tried to clear the high fence. By then

I had escaped the grasp of Sylvia and I ran towards the two of them. On route I picked up a five foot length of metal. I had just risked a limb with Sylvia and was not prepared to take any chances with a male version. I swung the bar towards the gypsy who was by then hanging over the top of the fence having had his escape interrupted by Frank Almond, who was clinging to his legs with some considerable difficulty. His spine made a perfect target and with no thought of a charge of grievous bodily harm or confining him to a wheelchair for the rest of his life, I struck him across his back, as hard as I could.

Apart from a gurgling scream and voicing a few choice words, due to the obvious pain, he showed no real discomfort and was able to kick his way free in the seconds it took me to rev up the enormous bar for a second swing. Away he went as nimble as ever, over the fence and out of sight as he bolted through the adjacent garden. I had more pressing problems and I was forced to turn and address Sylvia, who was by now screaming and bleeding profusely from a large gaping wound above her left eye. Frank continued the chase, having climbed the fence himself. I never thought for a moment he would catch the swift-footed gypsy and so didn't attempt to join in.

Dennis Williams, more of a diplomat than a fighter, was looking decidedly grey. His strong point was negotiation, not swinging metal bars. Diplomacy was however becoming difficult, even for Dennis to introduce into the situation. Sylvia's husband, known as Big Hughie, had seen the wound on his 'beloved' and was just returning from the house with a large knife. Big, as in Big Hughie, was an understatement. He was six foot six inches tall and just as broad with the reputation of being the family 'wildman.' In a family with Sylvia at the helm this was high praise indeed and an indication that he could be a prize psychopath. To say he was very angry seems somewhat obvious and irrelevant at this point. I was also pretty pissed off. Sylvia was getting blood on my Odermark jacket and wouldn't shut up screaming. She was also trying to kick me in the balls as I was again swinging the iron bar about, albeit in a half-hearted manner, more as defence than attack. I was, to say the least, very concerned about Big Hughie and was aware that I would have to use the bar in a much more positive fashion if he continued with his obvious intention of decapitating me.

Dennis, aware of the knife, bravely stood between the two of us and talked the situation down. Big Hughie was rightly upset at the assault and I agreed with him. This very rare moment of diplomacy had a calming effect on Hughie, just enough to realize he was about to murder a police officer and from a copper not known for such statements he took it all on board. Realizing this was the way forward and seeing the colour returning to Dennis' face I was on a roll and also apologized to Sylvia for the hasty action. This had an amazing effect. Despite the blood gushing from the open wound above her eye she was clearly touched in her own violent way. They had never had a police apology before and were immediately in unknown territory, and the situation calmed almost instantly. Big Hughie even chastised little Hughie for being cheeky to me having established he was out of range of my iron bar.

The divisional van arrived and amazingly it contained fearless Frank and the fleeing gypsy. By coincidence the van was driving through the area when they saw the chase. The blow with the bar had had more of an effect than I had realized. Frank actually caught the fleeing gypsy as the adrenalin wore off and the wounded man became increasingly aware of the excruciating pain in his lower ribs and back. Earlier in the chase the pain had not initially removed the ability to fight and he was able to give Frank a good hiding, before once again limping away and eventually being detained by the van crew who in true Biggest Gang fashion, jumped about on his already damaged ribs in the back of the wagon.

When back at the station the usual identification procedures were completed and the gypsy was identified and listed as wanted in the North East for a very serious assault. Officers from Newcastle travelled down to collect him and were rather impressed with the subservient rib-gripping welcome they got. Whilst allowing him to travel with the Newcastle officers we had not fully investigated the man and later established that he was also wanted on warrant in Manchester, which we then chose to ignore to hide our incompetence. The gypsy came to our attention again, some years later when he was shot in the North East and was in intensive care in a hospital. Our warrant came to light but we cancelled it in view of the circumstances. In the North East he had lost an arm in a gypsy shooting incident. He was however to be charged with a serious offence relating to grievous bodily harm, or attempted murder of the other party, once he had recovered sufficiently and was released from hospital. Our comparatively minor incident was not worth the trouble and the necessary paper work purely to have the sentence run concurrently with no benefit to us at all.

Whilst the paper work and wheels of justice were slowly turning and once everyone had been locked up and held in the cells, we returned to the garden and examined the metal with pound signs spinning in our eyes as in a Warner Brothers cartoon. The metal was loaded into the van, which on completion was so low with the weight that its tyres rubbed on the arches and the suspension was in great danger of total collapse.

Only a nominal amount of the metal was necessary as an exhibit. The Bullers pleaded guilty to handling the stolen material which was a lesser charge, claiming it to be stolen by the successful but bruised escapee who didn't care anyway.

As I said scrap dealers were a source of income. They bought recovered stolen metal at a little over the odds and also paid "rent' on a weekly basis for the privilege of being allowed to handle stolen property that hadn't been recovered by the local CID. They were usually visited on Saturday mornings when all the builders and plumbers were on their day off weighing in the week's proceeds and the scrap dealers were happy to pay to get the officers off the premises.

It is interesting to note that young Hughie grew up and became a force to contend with in the Moss Side and the

South Manchester underworld. I have no idea how successful he has been.

At the time I knew I was always in danger of one of Sylvia's gypsy curses which had a certain reputation for success. Whilst I would have not lost a lot of sleep about that, at the time I would have had a different view as the years have moved on. Due to a variety of circumstances I became a staunch believer in 'the other side' and the spirit world. When on nights I had actually seen what I believed to be ghosts in Didsbury Police Station, where several weird incidents had occurred probably because it used to be a funeral parlour many years earlier.

During my time in CID at Didsbury I was living in Cheadle Hulme, an upmarket area in the South of Manchester. The area used to be in Cheshire, but with the creation of Greater Manchester it acquired a Stockport postcode. This was to be the first house my wife and I purchased and it wasn't without a little assistance from various extra sources and totally accepted aspects of fundraising in the various departments I found myself in.

Within a very short period after the birth of my daughter we had a son. They were so close in age that they are the same age for three weeks every year as my son had a birthday three weeks before my daughter.

We had a dinner party for four guests when the children were babies and fast asleep upstairs. The dinner had been amply fuelled with homemade wine, which was a hobby of mine at the time. The wine and beer had flowed a little too much when the conversation turned to the spirit world and the other side. The guests were non-believers and I had already held some séances in Didsbury Station to take advantage of the fact that it used to be a funeral parlour. I had such success in speaking to the other side with what was a homemade Ouija board that caused hardened and initially disbelieving detectives to leave the room in some disarray. How they flinched and fled could certainly be described as fear, but that was always denied afterwards as it's quite a macho occupation as you are by now probably aware.

Perhaps it was ill advised, but it appeared perfectly sensible under the influence of my lethal homemade beverages, so we decided to have a séance. It was quite fashionable at the time to connect with the other side and Ouija boards had just appeared in the shops. I was confident that I had a guardian angel or at least a guiding light. As I moved on in my early life, I was confident that distant voices told me where I was going wrong. I used to talk to these voices and ignore them at my peril. I had tried this type of séance before and knew I could connect without any difficulty whatsoever, whether the lights were on and music played or not. Spirits don't need dark and they don't need quiet. Such props are only used for effect, to give a sinister ambience.

We tore pieces of paper into two inch squares and on them wrote every letter of the alphabet, and the numbers one through to 10. Two other papers bore the words YES and NO. They were all laid out on the table in a circle and we sat around in a circle. An upturned glass was placed in the centre and I put my forefinger on the base of the glass. Everybody laughed nervously with disbelief, but still they followed suit. I asked: "Is anybody there?" Nothing happened. But on the third time, same routine, the glass twitched. Everybody jumped, and the women, as usual, became all unhinged and jumped from the glass. One of them wouldn't return to the circle and decided to watch for who was causing the glass to move. I again asked: "Is anybody there?" The glass slid slowly to "Yes."

"Are you male?"

"Yes."

"Do you know anybody at the table?"

"No."

"Are you with someone who does?"

"Yes." We then had a sort of a conversation with the in-between. The conversation involved one of the girls in the séance and a distant great grandmother she barely knew of. Throughout, people were removing their fingers from the glass and trying to prove I was fabricating the connection. Finally only two of us had contact with the glass and it was still moving slowly until it eventually faded away as happens with faint contacts. The result was interesting but hardly conclusive. It was later proved the girl in question did have such a distant relative on her mother's side.

We continued with more fingers again on the glass and I again asked the question, adding, that if possible we would like to connect with someone, more closely connected with one of us at the table. This time we had a closer, stronger contact and the glass moved positively and with some force. The message was directed at me and claimed to be from a trumpeter at the Manchester Jazz Club in Long Millgate. I had never been there and didn't know the man. He told us he had died of a heroin overdose which was unusual in those days. Suddenly, the glass went wild and spelled out HAYES, CUNT, FUCKING BASTARD, and stopped. This was a shock. I knew I wasn't pretending and somewhere between obscenity and sensibility I established that the abusive individual was a regular at the Eighth Day, a shop and café on New Brown St before it was demolished to make way for the Arndale Shopping Centre. The contact was called Tony, a totally forgettable chap who had fallen foul of a couple of games of 'Drug Squad musical chairs' and certainly wasn't impressed. In the Drug Squad it was our practice to drive the addicts at the Eighth Day mad by planting drugs and arresting them. We believed it to be in their best interests as they could join a detox scheme if they wanted and get off the hard drugs and barbiturates to which they were addicted. Their kick was to take barbiturates and fight sleep and that had to be weird. This individual clearly blamed me for his demise as he had died of a drug overdose, taking too many barbiturates. We all looked at each other in shocked amazement. As my wife threw all the pieces of paper off the table and ran upstairs to the kids. I was concerned at this because I had read that if connection to the other side was not broken politely the spirit could remain in the property and clearly Tony was the last lodger we would want. He had gone and thankfully never returned.

I related this strange occurrence one night in the CID office and Dave Brodie, recently moved from Salford, frightened of nothing and nobody showed total incredulity. Some of the men present had already seen similar séances and were amused in anticipation of how Brodie would take it. The papers were written and circled, and once again I asked the question. As I have said already, Didsbury Police Station used to be a funeral directors and the neighbouring building remained so. This shouldn't have mattered as spirits tend to appear where they are happiest, or to people they are protecting, or at least watching over. We had taken a few drinks through the evening. Brodie was being light-hearted, but clearly a little nervous. The glass moved but there was continually such an inquest why it was happening that whatever spirits were there got well pissed off and threw the glass from the table as happens if they are not shown respect and taken seriously especially by a crowd of piss-heads.

Brodie continued to behave in a nervous childish manner, would not be sensible and appeared to be using this to cover his obvious fear and his dawning realization that there was something to be said for it after all. I was left little choice than to apologize to the spirits and discontinue.

THE EVER TIGHTENING NET OF INTERNAL DETECTION

The fittest and trickiest of us continued to ignore the pressures of the Complaints Department. Strangely this was known as the 'Y' Department. Perhaps it should have been spelt as 'why?' with the attached question mark. As the qualities of leadership at boss level waned and deteriorated we reached a point at which we were being led by the confused thinking of the glorified schoolboys at the helm. Once out of university they clearly realized that the pointed end on the rufty, tufty streets of Manchester was not really for them. It was a simple matter for them to spend a couple of initial years hiding in the police stations under the guise of completing paperwork and never actually making an arrest, or even dealing with an 'angry man.' Initially the Y department was formed, apparently for no other reason than to keep the lid on and prevent real police work and therefore any publicized embarrassment. Basically the more a working copper did, the more shit he fell into and so the work stopped and everyone went through the same old motions, so to speak of attempting to hide in the stations with the inevitable piece of paper.

Such a department initially flourished relying on fear and bullying, usually by men who themselves had never experienced real police work, never seen an angry man. They had never had to fight in a Yates' Wine Lodge, or had to fight their way out of a 'Black Power' unlicensed drinking establishment in Moss Side .

Such experience builds 'backbone', practical aptitude all thrown at you and the ability to lead from the front having been promoted through the ranks. Such hard work involving studying and policing rarely succeeded, but it was necessary to pass the often ridiculed promotion examination, which to be honest was never based on real police work and physical application. Examination questions were weird examples of ridiculous offences such as sheep shagging, incest and the theft of milk whilst indecently exposing oneself to a pensioner.

During my police service the examination consisted of three separate papers with numerous questions relating to subjects which, as I discovered later in my service, had little relevance to actual police work. I sat for the promotion examination to sergeant twice and on each occasion I had done little studying save for the one week course offered by the training school to thoughtfully assist with the style of the exam and the possible pitfalls. They could not however compensate for the overall lack of knowledge on so-called offences of which I had no practical experience. Based only on my actual practical knowledge, I failed on each occasion by only two points and realistically where would I be later in my police career had I made more effort. However, I can modestly say I was a great police officer at all levels. I was adept at the prevention and detection of crime as I was supposed to be, tempered with the abilities to avoid detection with regard to my extracurricular activities as with everyone else of the same generation.

As I went through my service I learned from many experienced serving officers the practical way the police should operate and not the text book version. The promotion examination did not differentiate between city and county forces, so it was common to have a detailed question relating to sheep dipping and what action to take in the event of an outbreak of myxomatosis in the pet rabbits at the local village school, or, of course, something else, equally as ludicrous and unlikely. The exam questions themselves were written in a manner that served no purpose in practicality in any case. A typical (and mildly tongue-in-cheek) example would read as follows:

A is a local farmer who has 100 sheep and 30 cattle. He has a shotgun without a certificate, because he has a previous conviction for being drunk and disorderly. He buys his cartridges from a friend B, who has a conviction for drunk driving. B owns a Land Rover and a tractor. A finds B having sex with one of his sheep whilst wearing A's wellingtons set aside for this purpose: to part the animal's rear legs, thus holding it steady for the sexual act. B did not have A's permission to take the boots or have sex with the sheep. A fired the shotgun into the hayloft of the barn where the act was taking place, with the intention of frightening B and perhaps occasioning a dislocation of the offending body part. Unknown to A his wife was having sex with B's 15-year-old son in the hayloft which collapsed with the impact of the shot onto B and the sheep. The sheep initially alarmed by the shot and then by the avalanche of hay and people, clenched its nether regions and ran from the barn taking with it the front of the wellingtons and part of B's anatomy.

B ran from the barn and drove his tractor from the private land of the farm onto the lane which was repairable at public expense, but without street lighting, to the nearest telephone box where he dialed 999 for an ambulance. He used obscene language when told to phone back later when the ambulance had returned from collecting the village policeman who had been knocked down by a stampeding ewe with what appeared to be balls hanging from its nether regions. The operator regarded the call as a hoax when B told her that the sheep's balls were actually his.

Discuss the offences revealed paying particular attention to the Telegraphy Act of 1872, the liberal use of obscene language by B and the offence committed by the operator.

Whilst this would appear to be a ludicrous examination question it is much closer to the truth than anybody other than an ex-police officer would suspect.

It is clear how university graduates were able to study for such examinations and be promoted ahead of the likes of working officers. It is equally clear how the police generally fell into the ruinous state it is in today, when such an important examination gives no serious regard to realistic or practical situations. At the time of my cadet service and later at training school questions such as this were taken seriously and nobody really questioned the dubious purpose and stupidity of it all.

It is interesting to note that the politicians found it necessary to introduce a Police Reform Bill in an attempt to show they had recognized the fact that the old "Fast Track" promotion scheme allowed "glorified children" direct from an early life of continual schooling until the age of 22, to accelerate through the ranks. They believe they have changed it all by introducing the HPDS (Higher Potential Development Scheme). This claims to give recruits the skills to progress more quickly to the ranks of sergeant and inspector and beyond through classroom training and practical policing.

Amazingly, it was believed that this new scheme was "fairer and better supported," whatever that means. A typical and recent newspaper article highlights the career of acting Inspector Stephen Barry who, from a photograph accompanying the article, it appears is barely out of short trousers. He actually admits he joined the police because of the Fast Track scheme. "It was a sweetener . . ." A typical admission, this proves that anyone is being accepted and instantly promoted. Inspector Barry studied Geology at university and will now, at police expense be funded for his postgraduate degree. He intends to take an MSc in Criminal Law at Brighton University. Am I actually from Mars or is it an incredibly childish belief by police leaders and politicians alike that this is experience that will stand him in good stead and give him the credibility that comes only with real experience. Politicians do not seem to grasp the fact that some things will never pass for experience. Men like this, these prospects for leading real men, need to be in a fight, especially a dirty one.

They need to lift a dead child, to render first aid to beaten women, an injured old aged pensioner, or tell a relative that their beloved has just been killed by yobs because the streets are unsafe. Some things must be lived through informative years of service. They cannot be taught in a classroom. Am I alone with my grumpy, but informed outlook? Am I alone with my outspoken comments that make it impossible for me to grasp how much a degree in Geology, or Domestic Science, or a subject equally removed from policing can prepare a candidate for service on the streets of any area of the United Kingdom? Do the same academics continue to believe there is actually 'life on Mars?'

However adept a policeman you once were, and they were becoming few and far between, there was also the need for the ability to study subjects which were unheard of with so many Acts and Sections and you had to know them to the point of perfection. Such a volume of necessary study meant that the police work suffered, that is to say with regard to those who actually attempted to fulfill such a requirement. The unofficial overtime, continued at the expense of the necessary study, often unpaid but lubricated with the free drink and food, readily available in many city establishments. All such activities continued to test the vagaries of the licensing laws, often misguided by the club owners who continued to believe that we still controlled the clubs and as long as they plied us with drinks all would be okay. It was not and such misguided thinking often resulted in prosecutions despite the bungs to various officers, which by now were being recognized as the rip-off they were by the club owners and proved on too many occasions to be all too difficult to convert into actual assistance with tip-offs and the like.

To make matters worse as the social life waned through lack of unofficial funding then so did the general freedom associated with our happy fun-filled days. Actual supervision was creeping in, but luckily it was mainly by the general pool of clueless university graduates and the like who had no real idea. These nine-to-five excuses for working police officers became the norm. Bureaucracy was taking over along with the almost endless admin needed to support such a useless volume of wasted staff. It quickly built to a point where as many men were stationed inside offices as were on the streets, or so it appeared. Departments sprung up for various minority groups such as pregnant lesbian officers, black officers and of course the newly appearing gay minority. Amidst all these unnecessary departments appeared a department which was titled the Inner City Liaison Department, which whilst geared to assist misguided children, allowed it to be manipulated by the many excuses for misguided children from their poor family backgrounds surrounded by drugs and often guns. This little 'mafia' was able to behave as it wished, even to throw stones at officers in the knowledge the kind Inspector, struggling with the lack of text books to cover the issues of 'mini scrotes,' would get them off and return them to their deprived family situation to watch the 50" telly, wipe cigarette smoke from their eyes and eat as many subsidized chips as they wished.

Leadership as it was loosely termed was based on so many men with no practical experience, leading the hard-nosed professionals from the desks at the rear whilst they continued to study and join various courses, often for 12 months at universities up and down the land. The aim for many was to pass yet more exams, obtain a degree in something equally useless and pass the equally pointless interviews.

The promotion ladder was based on passing the ridiculously complicated and difficult examination when a constable and then eventually being promoted to sergeant. From sergeant the same applied for promotion to inspector. In addition to passing the exam an interview was also part of the process. Interviews were headed by senior officers who had already passed through such a flawed system. At interview, questions based only on theory and inexperience were fired at the nervous applicant whose experience was generally at the same level and clearly easier to command, should they be promoted rather than the hard-nosed brigade who naively gave the correct answers born in the field, but totally none PC in the climate of the day. Admitting to planting evidence and 'persuading' a confession out of a prisoner were not the order of the day any longer. The actual men at the pointed end could not rely on absolute support, whatever the circumstances, from the so-called supervisory ranks.

The Y Department was eventually staffed by men boasting similar experience to that of ex-Chief Constable James Anderton. And Anderton himself clearly didn't realize the devastating effect the activities of the 'Y' would have on the 'worker bees' of the force, those who actually did something. Many quickly caught on to the dangers from so called colleagues that they faced and as a consequence refused to take the once normal risks of verballing, planting and general fabrication that came with the job and was seen as the norm. Now the risks were higher, but unnervingly they were all from the inside.

From such a festering process of inexperience and promotions appeared the Andertons, Bettisons of Hillsborough fame, Coyle of my murder investigation and Ralph Lees, who I first met as a cadet at Willert Street Police Station where he was the admin sergeant, stationed firmly behind a desk, shuffling papers, pettily resisting overtime claims of the overworked workforce, who were still willing to go the extra mile, provided the wages were paid. Times were changing and with them, many attitudes. These were attitudes forced on them by the stupidity from above and the lack of the social life bungs, which encouraged the leanings to real police work and extra time on the streets in the pursuit of justice.

On the subject of experience and "man for the job," I think it only right to highlight the position of Assistant Chief Constable Ralph Lees. This man was unbelievably, the head of CID. Stalker in his book describes him as "uncomfortable in that position." He must have started on the beat, was once an administrative sergeant and amazingly got promotion after promotion. This is a man who had been an administrator virtually all his service and was reputed to have hardly made an arrest and certainly not many in the last 25 years of his career as Stalker highlights in his book. Promoting men of this calibre to such positions effectively highlights reasons for men of the unquestionable quality and dedication of John Thorburn resigning as soon as possible.

At this time, the force had a thousand detectives and, in continuing with the theme of promoting inexperienced failures from such a wide choice, Anderton in his early days made Peter Topping a Detective Chief Superintendent and Lees his number two. Topping was later to become the head of CID and he spent a lot of his time digging for Keith Bennett, the victim of Ian Brady, over several years in a display of obsessive behaviour which should have given concern. He was effectively Anderton's puppet as of course was Lees, who was promoted even higher to Deputy Chief Constable. In effect these promotions were tantamount to the blind leading the blind. Stalker in his usual wet manner, further and unnecessarily polite, describes Lees as "markedly deficient in supervisory CID experience." What he should have said was that 'Lees would never be a detective whilst he had a hole in his arse!' Or am I being a little bit unkind in failing to spot all his obvious qualities.

At one stage such leadership failings and the poor end results were being recognized by the media, the general public and indeed by the Government of the day. As what was seen as a remedy the accelerated promotion procedure was introduced to attract officers leaving the army and university graduates all of whom were not prepared to walk the beat for a couple of years before even being able to sit the exam. In theory this would introduce new blood into the failing promotion procedures. I had always respected ex-army personnel, particularly those who had completed their National Service, during my days as a uniformed constable. They instilled a level of discipline at the time and it was thought that ex-officers would have a similar effect. Army officers later in my service were a slightly different breed, but still an improvement. Where, when and why university graduates came in to official thinking baffled us all. These were schoolchildren in long pants; they had grown in a cocoon of little study, heavy drinking, shagging and cannabis smoking.

Of course this bright idea failed to recognize that such men were to be leading with no experience of 'the streets' or life for that matter, as already existed in any case with the likes of Lees.

As I and the rest of the old school throughout the ranks struggled on with our belief that the public should be protected and crime should be detected whilst continuing to skate the thin blue line of honesty. Such a tenuous existence was necessary to improve on the continuing poor pay scales with various little scams, free lunches, bungs and the odd pardon.

It really was a lost cause as the vacuum of the experienced senior ranks retiring was continually being filled with the short-arsed inexperienced, chip-on-the-shoulder exam winners. By now the height requirement had been reduced to 5'6" in some forces. Seeing such a man swaggering about a city, under an ill-fitting helmet, draped over the ears, adorned in all the self-preservation equipment provided little comfort to the public at large as they pushed on with the them and us wedge of the hierarchy, which now separates the public and the untouchable and badly-led police of today. The lack of ability for confrontation in aggressive situations came with such height deficiencies and levels of cowardice appeared at so many levels. Such officers were clearly nervous of the 'pointed end' and experienced officers who were not afraid to speak their mind continually reminded them of their failings and the fact that they didn't have the balls to instill any semblance of discipline which of course built respect. Such weak supervision further eroded the very fabric of real police work and whatever shreds of respect that still existed were quickly eroded as these poor excuses quickly gave cowardly priority to easy prosecutions, which soon became the order of the day.

Parking and speeding offences resulted in the reducing number of arrests for disorderly and anti-social behaviour. The many cowardly officers with no respect on the lawless council estates happily hid away in their various nicks, completing the masses of paperwork associated with a parking prosecution. Anderton in yet another attempt at headline-grabbing decided to raid all the 'dirty book shops' in Manchester and rid the streets of such filth. Such failings in pro-active policing left the streets to be a quagmire of scrotes and professional unemployed criminals, mugging pensioners and generally forcing the public at large to remain in their homes after dark in what were rapidly becoming unpoliced council estates. The term, police was swiftly becoming a joke, with no respect whatsoever except from the older generation who continued to give their unwavering support until such a time that they had cause to dial 999 for assistance which never came.

It's no surprise that one of a moronic band of swaggering shitbags revelling in the name the Benchill Mad Dogs had the audacity to pretend to point a gun at the then opposition leader 'Call Me Dave' Cameron on a visit to Manchester's Wythenshawe Estate just a couple of years ago. The brain-dead moron and his idiot cronies even bragged about their behaviour to The Sun, safe in the knowledge that they believed the police had lost the plot and were no longer in charge of the streets. The rise of the short policeman inevitably led to a shrinking of the long arm of the law.

Dirty little tricks...the continuing culture

Without doubt the biggest, most interesting and complicated prosecution I had ever been involved in, started simply enough. It began with a phone call from a bed and breakfast hotel in Withington, an area of bedsits and small hotels on Wilmslow Road, an arterial route running from the city centre, out through Didsbury and on to Manchester International Airport. A chambermaid had been tidying a room and found two bullets. The guest was having breakfast. Today a special armed unit would have been turned out, Wilmslow Road would have been closed for hours whilst helmeted marksman surrounded the building to allow a negotiator to shout through a megaphone and insist on surrender.

We didn't have any guns. We didn't really tell anyone where we were going. Dennis Williams and I took the office car from someone who was attempting to conceal the keys and we drove to Withington, only four miles away. In typical fashion I used the call as an excuse to drive like an absolute lunatic, through the rush hour traffic. The hotel was a large four storey semi-detached building, a guesthouse actually. The reception desk was near the front door and the dining room was, effectively, the bay windowed front room. Our man was identified by the staff who cowered behind the reception desk out of sight of the guest. He was seated alone in the bay window, as far from the door as he could have been. We moved quickly into the room, me at the front, Dennis doing a "George Dampier," as it was known in repeated diplomatic renditions of the IRA raid from my Drug Squad days. The guest reacted immediately, clearly realizing we were police and heading for him, he made an attempt to stand, as he did so putting his right hand into the inside of his jacket. You can imagine my thoughts and the words I used mentally as I ran at him. The call was regarding bullets and here was the suspect putting his hand into his pocket as I approached at speed. I realized that I could be the headlines in the late edition of the Manchester Evening News. I hit him with the full force of several years of rugby playing and amateur wrestling as he was withdrawing his hand from his jacket. The breakfast went everywhere. The guest went through the window with me, onto the car park. He found breathing extremely difficult for many minutes, having cushioned my fall very effectively.

The idea of calling an ambulance was quickly forgotten and we dragged him screaming and wheezing to his feet. We established that he was attempting to remove a gun, which was actually a starting pistol with tear gas capsules that would have blinded anyone close enough when fired. The bullets found in the room by the chambermaid were real, but there was no trace of an actual firearm. This incident could have been extremely embarrassing had it proved to be a copy of "War Cry" he was removing from his pocket, but the situation didn't allow for any hesitation whatsoever. His room was searched and so was he. There was nothing else incriminating in the room. He was, however, carrying a locked briefcase which he had with him at breakfast, but appeared to have no key.

We took him back to Didsbury and sat him in the rear interview room. Having searched him loosely at the hotel to establish if he had any other weapons in his pockets, we searched him properly, stripped him off and in doing so found a key on a string around his neck. It opened the briefcase and to our unforgettable amazement this was full of £5 postal orders, £20 notes, blank motor vehicle logbooks, some pornography and invoices for several printing accessories. On closer inspection the bank notes, the postal orders and the log books were found to be expertly forged. It was immediately clear that this was a significant find. From the information and the invoices in the briefcase we established an address for a printing works in Ancoats, an area of central Manchester.

Eric Jones, immediately on the ball and the real detective he was, recruited several other members of staff and we all raided the printing works. On entering we saw that the premises housed a real printing operation. They had many machines and printing plates, piles of blank paper and inks. There were several completed orders, involving commercial contracts for mass repeat printing of brochures and letterheads piled near the exit awaiting delivery. There were several members of staff all clearly with their own positions at various machines and indeed a hive of honest industry. They were very surprised at our intrusion and as we examined all the machines and completed stock we could see that there was not a trace of forged notes, log books or postal orders. They were all arrested and removed to the station whilst a detailed search took place. Having interviewed the innocent members of the staff we established that the firm undertook regular printing contracts in the day and then they thought it was used at night, but not by any of the day staff. Some of them believed that forgery was taking place, because they often found scrap traces and accessories which had not been hidden away. The fear of detection had never appeared to have been a factor. The night staff never considered that such an eventuality was a real possibility and often astonishingly never cleared away the traces of the night's work.

The method of forgery was ingenious or, at least, it was ingenious to us. To print a twenty pound note a photograph of the note would be taken with filters on the cameras to coincide with the five colours in the note. A printing plate for each colour was then prepared. This was repeated for every colour in the note. Each plate was then used on a simple photo lithographic printing machine to print its corresponding colour on quality bank note paper. Each plate was then changed as was the colour and a second plate was run over the existing paper, which bore the first image. It was vital that each plate was set up perfectly, identical to the previous one so that the images were perfectly clear and sharp. Each colour run was of thousands of sheets, with thousands of full colour notes as the end product. The watermark was added as the final touch with clear ink. The black line which was to resemble the silver strip line, when viewed through the paper was added and then the entire process was repeated on the other side and again the setup had to be incredibly accurate. The postal orders were printed with a similar process with much less effort and the log books were hardly a challenge, being a simple printing process on the appropriate paper. Log books at this time were simpler documents, which started as an A4 piece of thick green paper that was then folded into a small booklet.

This was clearly a very simple though potentially massive operation and our action prevented it from ever taking final shape. On closer examination over the days we spent at the works we found several discarded printing plates and partially printed scrap paper by the bundle as the alignment process had failed. The interviews of the principal and the staff were lengthy and resulted in the identification of other individuals who were also arrested. Eventually we discovered that this very efficient fraud was actually in its 'infancy' and at the very start of its operation.

Few of the bank notes and postal orders ever appeared on the open market, except for the few which were skimmed at the time of the search, by the investigating hordes enlisted earlier at Didsbury, just to prop up the drinking fund at the Royal Oak. The printer, Peter Foss, a German national, knew the game was up, but was not entirely cooperative. Of course, he realized that whatever he did say would only make matters worse for him and wasn't stupid enough to believe that all the help he gave would be taken into account at court as promised. He was interviewed several times and many exhibits were seized. Inspector Eric Jones led the prosecution preparation. His aptitude for organization and order came to the fore with this incident. Dennis Williams and I were taken off regular duties and given our own incident room at Platt Lane Police Station. It was a larger station and the only one that had spare rooms. I was appointed to the venerable position of exhibits officer and believe it or not, in an investigation of this magnitude it was actually an important position where attention to detail was vital.

For the purposes of evidential continuity, every single exhibit had to be logged and labelled with the time and date where it was found and by whom. They were all bagged and initially many items were just grabbed and stuffed in one bin liner and humped to Didsbury. By the time the seized items which proved to be of evidential value were recognized as important, they had been piled altogether in the middle of the floor. As the days went on, the interesting items were bagged and labelled and the evidence would be that this had been meticulously completed at the printing works for the vital continuity. On at least two occasions a crucial piece of evidence would be found after the lengthy list of consecutively numbered exhibits had been recorded. Should the continuity of these particular items be of such importance the original list would have to be rewritten, the labels destroyed and every item numbered again. Admittedly testing the laws of evidence, but totally necessary. We searched Foss' home and eventually discovered the gun that the bullets found at the hotel fitted. It was a large automatic pistol and, despite being declared a part-time marksman, I had never handled such a gun. I opened the magazine. It was empty. I replaced the magazine, cocked the mechanism and pointed the gun in the general direction of the side of the room where Foss was sitting. I pulled the trigger, the gun clicked. I cocked the mechanism in true Dirty Harry style, only childishly playing at cowboys when a bullet popped out of the upper chamber. The room occupied by several seasoned detectives fell to a hush that is apart from the strained gasping of air in disbelief. Not a word was spoken until my quivering 'fucking hell' accompanied by a hysterical giggle broke the ice. By this time I felt dizzy and my arse went into my throat as Eric collapsed into a chair and looked towards Foss who wasn't really phased by it at all.

Foss was resigned to the rest of his life in prison, so dying didn't seem so terrible at the time. He barely reacted and was amused at the reaction from the assembled officers. We carried on as though nothing untoward had happened. Foss was German. Perhaps his history allowed for such behaviour, sanctioned at the time by Hitler, the SS, and the German police. However for such a potentially serious incident to occur in leafy Didsbury village was not really in keeping with the tranquil existence we loved and abused.

Over the following weeks and months we prepared the case. The exhibits were labelled and bagged by the tens and then hundreds as we progressed. On a further couple of occasions the labelling and bagging had to be reviewed as a rogue exhibit appeared, perhaps from a car boot where it had remained undetected until the car had a puncture. It had to be slotted in with total continuity and should a few labels require rewriting once again, then so be it. As we progressed several other lesser villains were dragged into the possession of forged instruments "net," particularly the members of the motor trade who regarded the log books as manna from heaven. During the detailed investigation we conducted many interviews and throughout never identified a financier for Foss, though we believed one existed. Eventually despite a total silence from the arrested numbers we eventually thought we had found the ringleader and financier of the entire operation, but had little real evidence to help a prosecution. Dennis Williams' crystal ball would not really hold up at Manchester Crown Court as evidence. Enid Blyton was going to have to make an appearance. All three of us were known to have a 'wicked' pen and we all vied for the position of Enid Mark 1. The end result of perfectly-written yet inventive prose would have to be excellent, but, initially, required some assistance.

To give the intended verbals a little credibility, some added authentic forensic evidence was necessary to provide an interview with a theme for discussion. A car belonging to 'Mr Big' was seized and was adapted with a little evidence that would be found forensically, by the forensic scientists who were to take the car apart in their search for clues. During these years of forensic examination, there were many tests that had not been discovered, DNA just one of many not available. The chemists did their best as they saw it, but we had little faith in these wizards from the laboratory in Chorley, Lancashire. Instead there were a couple of what we regarded as miniscule but obvious 'clues.' These would, therefore be traced to the same papers and inks used in the forgery at the print works. The car was delivered to the laboratory and returned back to us a fortnight later by a member of the lab staff with a very wry smile. Nothing had been found in relation to the items we had added, which of course would have been impossible in reality. It was very disappointing that the lab had seen through our ruse, but worth a chance in our eyes. And we thought we had been so clever.

It was a common practice to fabricate forensic evidence, as it is today, to assist a rather poor case. Probably more so today, being bound by the rules for a tape-recorded interview, so there has to be another source of irrefutable evidence. In searches of suspects' houses, shoes are seized and returned having been used to prepare a footprint at the scene to be found later. Soil samples can then be taken and compared to those on the shoes and at the scene. There have been several convictions overturned in the last few years, where such police tactics are no longer believed and where forensic evidence is found to be the only proof, the conviction is ruled as unsafe. Another simple but common forensic ruse was the finding of hair samples in a hat or balaclava abandoned at a crime scene. Often hairs are removed from combs and brushes at a suspect's home and then later found in the balaclava helmets and so on and so on. Another popular forensic 'find' is that of gunshot residue on the hands and sleeves of any suspect, evidence easily developed just by firing a pistol.

When I left the police and was in my capacity of private eye I used to offer a service of preparing defences. One such case involved a man arrested for a bookmaker's robbery, where he was alleged to have climbed over the front metal grille on the counter. There was little real evidence in the case and forensic examination was used. Strands of fibres were 'luckily' found on top of the bars, apparently detached by friction as the robber climbed over. The suspect was, of course, to have been found in possession of a pair of trousers with the same fibre. He was found not guilty when I outlined the practice of assisted forensic evidence at court. This fibre was used in the manufacture of millions of pairs of trousers by many other manufacturers. A fact the police had failed to mention.

Meanwhile, back in the forgery case the preparation of the prosecution went well and Foss and company pleaded not guilty on solicitor's advice. They didn't have a chance, but this was such a good earner for the law firms on the Legal Aid system that a guilty plea would have meant one day at court, but still at a cost of tens of thousands of pounds. Each defendant had a QC and a junior barrister at a cost of about £5,000 a day in a trial which lasted the best part of a month.

The process of giving evidence in British courts is very strict and has to be seen as fair by the trusting public, particularly by those doing their duty on a jury. Each witness remains outside of court until his evidence is required. In the forgery case I had made a lengthy statement of evidence in relation to the arrest and preparation of the exhibits. The system would be that the court usher inside the courtroom would find the exhibit and produce it to the judge and the counsel before showing it to the jury, all 12 of them. In barely an hour the judge became so pissed off with the dithering usher and the fact he could not read most of the labels written quite hurriedly on the fourth attempt and he had failed to take in the numerical order and the manner of display I had described. Despite my detailed explanation of the system I had introduced and indeed was very proud of, the usher was unable to grasp the situation and as a consequence was panicking and rooting about randomly in all 800 exhibits. The unprecedented decision was made by the judge and all the barristers for the defence and the prosecution that I should be allowed to remain in court and produce the exhibits as named in other witness' evidence. Once again the wheels of justice changed direction purely to suit a judge. This worked perfectly and whilst I sat happily in court listening to the cross examinations of Dennis Williams and Eric Jones, I was able to identify any difficult questions that were to be directed at me well beforehand and so formulate the necessary evidence in my mind. As the trial progressed it was clear that there would be no embarrassing questions. The entire trial was just a formality and the barristers for the prisoners even had a drink with us occasionally after the day's court. On one occasion I remember Foss' barrister, the celebrated George Carman, taking a double gin and tonic in his stride and saying: "You know Mr Hayes, you are fucking mentally ill!" And then George guffawed with Eric Jones, who was also laughing, and totally impressed with his powers of deduction and evidently in total agreement.

I assumed he was referring to the pistol incident, which clearly had been mentioned by Foss to his barrister but never used at the trial. Foss was in enough bother without actually having the temerity to accuse a servant of the Queen of such a potentially violent act. Today, accused persons appear to attempt every trick in the book, but during those times, malicious and improbable accusations were never introduced.

Another incident Foss decided never to mention was an act of charity on the part of Dennis Williams the supervising sergeant during his transportation from Didsbury to the cells at Longsight, where he was duly charged with a few simple holding charges until the full case could be prepared. During the journey Foss asked to go for a drink, being totally confident that he would hardly see the light of day for some time as the offence of forgery carried a long sentence being committed against the Crown. In his possession he had about fifty pounds and insisted we spent most of it in a small pub in Rusholme on route. During this time and whilst standing at the bar Foss was happily handcuffed to me, whilst Dennis purchased the beers. Fifty pounds during these wonderful years took some spending and Foss was hardly able to stand as he was processed through the charging system. The trial eventually came to an end. Foss was found guilty and sentenced to 20 years in prison. Throughout the interviews Foss had always admitted to the offences and was happy to plead guilty and would certainly have been sentenced to less had he pleaded so. His legal advisors failed to mention that minor detail. What did they care? They certainly made no reference to the excessive fees they were to earn as a result of the lengthy trial. A couple of years ago, I heard Foss was out of prison and printing again. Apparently it was as in the old days and clearly if I had heard of it just around Manchester like so many other rumours and questionable tales. But if I'd heard of it then so would all the snouts in the city and surely Peter Foss would be making a return visit to Strangeways if at all true and that's not happened as far as I am aware. Manchester is a village as silly as it seems and gossip runs amok and so it may all be nonsense.

George Carman was also the celebrated Queen's Counsel in the 1979 Jeremy Thorpe 'biting the pillow' defence and so many more, including Ken Dodd's tax trial. Gorgeous George was a bon vivant, a serious drinker and lived on the Didsbury section. He was occasionally in the Royal Oak and always joined us to lambast us in his amazing style about some perjury or other. He would often telephone the nick with: "This is Mr Carman. Is that lunatic Hayes on duty and if so I want to see him?" George was better kept onside and we would entertain him wherever possible. In entertain I mean, we would collect him, drive him to chosen hostelries and he would pay for the drinks all night. I was one of the few who could keep up with his treble gin and tonics. How he could perform in any court the following day with such a sharp mind amazed everyone. My pal George lived in a strange large Victorian semi of three storeys. He had a much younger wife who I recall had something of a hippy style. I was never invited in, but could clearly see that the hallway was painted black.

Didsbury continued to be an upper class area where time- served Manchester citizens preferred to reside as opposed to moving out to Wilmslow, or Hale, in Cheshire.

We had the Lord Mayor voted in for a year residing on Spath Road and we were expected to visit his home through the evening and night to make sure his wife was safe whenever he was out at a function or on other council business. It was all PR and all that was required was a call to the nick to have the property shown as for 'special attention.' This ensured the Lord Mayor got the same attention as the local peep show, which whilst not as rewarding had to be done.

I'll never forget driving the car with Sergeant Albert Yates one night. Albert was a neighbour of mine in Cheadle Hulme and had a different outlook on police work to me. He was ex-Special Branch and had got into the habit of doing little. We had been invited to a local hostelry to attend the launch of Carlsberg Special Draught Lager, a cheeky little creation which rolled off the tongue like a steam roller. We were both horrendously pissed and to make it worse I was driving.

Drunk driving was never an issue to be concerned about, but this beer was strong and the likelihood of a miscalculation increased. We arrived at the Lord Mayor's house and the bedroom light was on as the Lady Mayoress was about to retire. She must have heard the horrendously pissed Detective Sergeant Yates struggling to get out of the car. We had a police radio which was secured to the glove shelf with a transmitter similar to a telephone attached by a long length of spiralled wire. Albert had his right foot tangled in the cable of the radio and as he staggered from the vehicle, attempting to kick the wire from his feet he fell and as he did so he dragged the entire radio fitting, parcel shelf and all out of the car. He managed to get to his feet and walked in what he regarded as a confident style, but tending to lurch to the right then the left in an uncontrolled manner as he attempted to keep his balance. Ever confident and insisting on completing the visit he staggered into the front garden, stood below the bedroom window and looked up at the sash which had by then been opened by a bemused Ladyship leaning out somewhat perplexed.

With a slur she was greeted by: "Sergeant Yates from the CID ma'am, just seeing if you are okay?" Looking ever more confused and quizzical she confirmed she was, so hurriedly went back inside before she was forced to understand a further barrage of what she felt she recognized as 'Mongolian.' Albert's brain, his legs and his balance had completely lost any agreement between themselves and the act of looking up to the first floor window didn't help. Albert did what appeared to be a half-hearted Double Salko, scoring only three, before falling backwards into the rose bushes. I can't really say I was much steadier than Albert, but managed to drag him from the roses and pile him and the demolished radio back into the car and return to the nick so he could sleep it off.

Albert Yates never looked back. As he so readily proved he was able to adapt to the brigade of YES men and aspired through the ranks. When I left the police, I was informed by a close friend of Albert, which indeed I thought I was, that he was actually jealous of my success and objected to the fact that he remained in his little semi in Cheadle Hulme, whilst I climbed the property ladder fuelled by my private detective agency success. It appears he has now improved his situation with a substantial property above Hollingworth Lake close to Rochdale.

I am told he even tried to have me investigated, never believing I was actually earning an honest living and consequently afforded the lifestyle I constantly rammed down the throats of my ex-colleagues. Lazy people, I had worked with in the police could never understand how people succeeded by working 16 hours a day and having earned the money, spent every penny giving the impression of a lavish lifestyle, which indeed I suppose it was.

When at Didsbury and serving together Albert and myself had a reasonable working relationship, but the social life was much better. We both frequented the same licensed premises and went out with the same group of women. They were all barmaids, usually married and mine seeking only casual sex, either in a car, the office flat whilst it existed, or on the boss' new carpet.

One sunny morning we both went to a suspicious incident, where a man thought to be asleep but in some difficulty, was sitting upright and motionless in a car on Fog Lane about a mile from Didsbury Police Station. His eyes were barely open, but he was motionless. The car door was open and it didn't take a doctor to see he was dead. We called the force doctor for the area and Eric Jones appeared on the scene. Not in his capacity as medical advisor, simply as a nosey bastard seeking something different to tidy up. We had the car taped off and the surrounding area. As every dead body is regarded as suspicious until a doctor says otherwise. Initially, it was treated as a murder investigation. This meant everyone stood around, took some notes as the log of the incident and disappeared behind the screens which had been hurriedly delivered in what I thought was a rare display of efficiency and urgency by a support team. The speedy erection of the screens immediately prevented the local schoolchildren talking to the body and poking him for dares.

The doctor arrived and pronounced him dead, making an odd assessment concerning the degree of rigor mortis. It appeared he had been dead for about six hours. Rigor mortis is a condition the body assumes after being dead for some time. After dying, it stays limp and then goes hard at every joint before going limp again. With the body remaining in the car for so long, it had once again stiffened in the pose it maintained at the wheel. The car was a Reliant Scimitar. The two seats in this sports car were of the bucket type and the driver sat in what was basically an upholstered trench. His hands were holding the wheel tightly, his eyes were open and staring and the face still had an appearance that he had died in some pain.

The doctor could do little. He authorized the body to be removed to the mortuary for a full post mortem examination to establish the cause of death. It was believed he had suffered a heart attack, but, at this stage, his death could of course have happened due to several reasons, even poisoning, or some other invisible cause. Removing the body was easier said than done and certainly not as simple as the doctor presumed. The fingers, still grasping the wheel in his final death throes had to be prised open and with a couple broken we had to pry them from the wheel. The body was already decomposing and smelling. We then had to get the rigid 15 stones out of the trench and through the door of the car. Had he been soft and bendable it would have been much simpler. The removal proved nigh on impossible, because the body couldn't be bent sideways, or in any direction to facilitate extraction from the seat. Pulling him out was not practical, as he was wedged in and to make matters worse, every time we moved the body, gas erupted from every orifice as the decomposition set in. Before this exercise was even attempted, the car smelt of death. What exactly it smelt off after this little episode I am not really sure.

It's hard to explain the smell of death. It is not particularly pungent, but it lingers, and the smell remains with you forever. The smell returns in the nostrils many days after, even if every stitch of clothing you wore at the time had been changed and cleaned. The smell of the gas is not so bearable and some of us were having difficulty keeping the previous night's six pints and curry in place. The only way forward was to ensure the screens were well in place and the public had no view at all. We decided on an acrobatic type of removal. I was supported from the passenger side and pushed with my legs on the body's arm and shoulder and as it started to lean through the doorway, farting and squelching I pushed on the hips until the entire body spiralled out of the car, like a party balloon, being supported by about four retching assistants. He was placed in the black and anonymous mortuary van and taken to the morgue.

The public entrance to the morgue was clean and efficient. It always had the strong smell of disinfectant to hide the inevitable smell of death. It had a comfortable waiting area, with wooden panelling, a plaque denoting the date when it was opened, a vase of flowers and a sliding glass window for the receptionist to greet the public through. A woman specially chosen for having the sour appearance of someone having just eaten a lemon, suitably dour and respectful. From the waiting area was a door which led to another room divided by a large glass panel. Behind this panel bodies were shown for formal identification to relatives and others. If not for the glass panel relatives inevitably threw themselves on the body, hugging and kissing and proving impossible to remove. A member of staff, adept at the art of cosmetics, would pad out the faces and make up the body to resemble the person they once knew. This is an art and, unfortunately, the artist at the time must have just returned from a season with Coco the Clown. I had seen dead bodies which actually appeared to be alive but some efforts were very poor and as a consequence very upsetting for the relatives.

We entered the morgue by the tradesmen's entrance, which was a large sliding metal door from the enclosed yard at the rear of the building. The smell hits you immediately and despite the caustic solutions used for cleaning and sterilizing, the smell of death and dissected guts was everywhere. In the main room was a wall of metal drawers big enough to accommodate a body on a stretcher. There were about 50 drawers. The entire wall was a fridge. Each drawer was labelled and the bodies interred therein were awaiting post-mortem examination, identification, or removal by the funeral directors. The post-mortems were carried out in the same room on white enamel tables with a raised irrigated rim which prevented the body parts falling on the floor. This also allowed the blood and later the cleaning fluid to run away easily. The tables had the appearance of flat baths and were equipped with taps, a hose and strong lighting above. There were several tables all of which were occupied by bodies in various stages of decomposition. A couple of them had the top of the head removed. Others had the entire ribcage split open to reveal the contents of the chest and abdomen. I don't think we can ever realize how long our bowels are until they are laid out around a mortuary table awaiting dissection. These appear to be the first part of the body to expand with gas and when dissection of these occurs, the uninitiated certainly need a gas mask, but usually aren't wearing one so regularly vomit all over the floor.

The principal in charge of the morgue is the physician who undertakes the actual post-mortem. He is medically qualified and on this occasion happened to be a man appropriately named Blench. Blench? Look it up. He was small in stature, wore spectacles and always had a short cigarette burning in his mouth. He was a chain smoker but, strangely he was never seen to light up, or put the cig out and yet the cigarette was always half-smoked. He only stopped smoking to eat a sandwich, which he kept on a side table rather than leave his post.

He wore a large green apron and cap, which were always smothered in blood and guts. His notes were dictated into an overhead microphone for typing later. Once he had completed the post mortem, he moved on to the next, whilst the body was sewn back up by an assistant with the same level of expertise as the makeup artist. Whatever exhibits were needed to confirm the cause of death would be safely bottled in a special fluid. The remainder were thrown back into the body cavity and sewn up. The table was then washed down and the next body laid out for examination.

All the real labour in the morgue was performed by men who appeared to have failed the auditions for the Addams Family. It appeared some had been chosen for their sickly smiles and staring goldfish eyes. There have been many instances of such attendants having sex with the inmates of morgues and, even during my service, at least two were charged. It was rumoured that Jimmy Savile got up to the very same trick when he helped out in the morgue at Stoke Mandeville. Even his former BBC DJ colleague Paul Gambaccini reckoned the filthy pervert was also a necrophiliac. Whenever we visited the morgue, they took exceptional delight in opening a drawer to show off a 'pretty one.' To this day I wonder if the sex they had with the bodies was with or without make-up?

Our driver was identified as Horace somebody and he was balanced on one of the tables because they couldn't get him in a drawer. He could not be pushed flat until the post mortem had taken place. He was still effectively in a seated position and when laid on his lower back, he pivoted at this area and was perfectly balanced with his arms still out in front of him and his legs at a similar driving angle. The attendants had attempted to cover him in a sheet.

The morgue is often being visited by trainee constables and cadets in a tour of various establishments of interest. The staff there took great delight at presenting a length of bowel or a hand concealed in a sleeve, offered as a handshake to some young policewoman whilst several of her colleagues were becoming reacquainted with their breakfasts. A couple of these stood to the side of Horace who was still covered by the sheet where it touched, with the odd arm and leg protruding. Albert Yates turned to the body and said: "What do you think of it all up to now, Horace?" As he did so, he pushed down gently on one of the feet and through closed lips shouted: "Rubbish!" As Horace, wide-eyed, sat up, looking for all the world to have come back from the dead. As we collapsed in fits of disrespectful laughter the herd of trainees all chose to huddle together some yards away, which in itself caused further mirth.

I remember one incident when I was on the evening crime patrol for the D Division. The evening crime patrol was a rather ingenious shift to ensure that at least two detectives were in contact with police work, should the rest of the division be partying in their various chosen hostelries. In theory, it worked. In practice the jury is still out.

Again when visiting the mortuary we found that a young policewoman was unconscious on the floor, accompanied by two laughing colleagues and the suspect mortuary attendants. These chaps were just delighted at any horizontal female whether dead or alive. In the knowledge that they were to attend the mortuary, one of the WPC's male colleagues had gone ahead and was put in a drawer by the attendants. On arrival of the policewoman the drawers were opened, as though to seek a particular body. When the drawer with the PC inside was opened, he sat up, moaned "yes" and watched as the WPC collapsed to the floor.

Light-hearted moments such as these helped ease the strain and loosen the tight wires of the more difficult part of the job, none more difficult than informing a relative or loved one of the sudden death of someone close to them, especially in the knowledge of the procedures at the morgue.

And there's almost an end

Being on a division out of the city centre presented several different areas that I was not acquainted with. Every serving police officer whether in uniform or CID in every department I have served always searched for something, anything that was free and in reality should not have been unless it was to benefit the officer concerned.

All manner of freebies were the targets. On the simple and easy to get spectrum were the pubs, clubs, and restaurants, where unlimited drink and food was on offer. It was not always freely given until a fault was found in the conduct of that particular business, even if only parking outside a restaurant on the footpath for example, or even a variety of relatively serious situations regarding possibly the use of and even the sale of drugs. Dealers were allowed to operate for the usual agreed rent. Pubs were allowed to remain open for business despite the rigid licensing laws, often through the night in certain circumstances. All variety of criminal activities were permitted, office pardons given when caught and right up the table to actually committing the crime.

On the city centre A Division, the closest to "honest" crime actually was and probably still is, the return of shoplifting goods. This proved to be a realistic source of income with little danger of any comeback, as the only complaint could come from the store detective who was also at the centre of this activity. On the D Division there were only a few shoplifters, but a replacement source of income surfaced. Though totally distasteful this new earner was pursued with vigour by more officers than would ever be presumed. Elderly people have always had a mistrust of banks and in Wythenshawe were inevitably mugged on the journey home having drawn a few quid. They chose to keep the money in the house, concealed in a variety of places which they considered secure, such as in newspaper under the carpet or lino. Attached to the back of sideboard drawers was another favourite and of course under the mattress. Items of jewellery were concealed in a similar manner. Many old people led a lonely life in Wythenshawe and passed away without anyone noticing, or them being missed at all. They were not missed for days, even weeks. The thoughts of close family units, regular care visits and concerned grown-up children were not factors in their miserable existences. The body would simply lie decomposing in the house, often with a pet which decided to live on the owner rather than starve to death.

As when I initially joined the city centre CID I innocently believed that no one would want such menial tasks as arresting shoplifters, but they were massively popular arrests. I saw the CID as an illustrious body and believed that nobody would want part of such a petty and boring task. I was sure seasoned detectives would avoid such a duty and yet there were nearly blows exchanged to attend such a petty arrest. It took me some weeks to understand this rather bizarre practice when at Bootle Street CID. It was certainly a greater secret than the masonic ritual of membership. Similar values appeared to reign with regard to the investigation of sudden deaths. Not murders but elderly people, simply passing away in their homes.

Looking back it took me some time to realize. Of course I was suspicious as detectives with no reputation at all for real police work were once again practically fighting for the completion of the death report. I soon enough established that my suspicions were well-founded and that there was an art involved. In the Drug Squad I was one of the gifted members who could pick up the smell of cannabis resin, however well it was concealed. Incredibly typical searches were initially for the smell of money. It certainly had a smell all of its own and became increasingly strong when kept in a concealed place and with practice could be detected above the stench of a decomposing corpse. Stashed, hidden money that nobody would miss as nobody knew it was there. The house was searched under the pretext of looking for the relatives' details, but in reality, the hidden money was being sought and certainly not for the forthcoming probate. However original the elderly people thought they were, they were acting on ages-old traditions, where everyone had access to others' homes, keys were left under doormats and the door wide open when in the house. Cash was always found in biscuit tins, under the carpet, in a Tupperware box in the fridge and under the good old mattress. Relatives when they eventually attended, with petty greed written all over their faces, were very regularly rather disappointed. They also clearly believed that money was hidden and wanted to search. They could have done in most instances, but to aggravate the wanton greed etched on their little faces and just to be awkward they were messed about and prevented with claims that it was still the scene of a possibly suspicious death. They had never visited the lonely elderly relative when alive and suddenly they cared. In any case they were never in the actual race, as the search had already been exhausted well before they were informed and then due to the passage of travelling time they had no chance and their petty little wrinkled smokers' faces continued to distort in the hope they would find something.

As well as the readies the found property bonus often included family jewellery and some of that could be very valuable. There were often previously unrecognized antiques in such houses and each division had its own road show of antiques experts. A death, simple death, however sad, also offered innumerable other possibilities. It was common practice for officers to actually work at funeral directors, washing and preparing bodies, driving the hearse and carrying the coffin into the church as pall bearers. I recall the worshipped former Manchester United manager Sir Matt Busby having his coffin robbed by one of the pall bearers from his funeral. At the time the thief lived in Wythenshawe, but found himself on the front page of The Sun when he tried to sell pictures of Sir Matt in his coffin. When dealing with the relatives, officers would assist as they could in suggesting all the necessary support services, which go with a funeral. The helpful suggestion of an appropriate florist usually ensured receiving a suitable bouquet for "the wife."

Not particularly connected to this, but just something that comes to mind now is a memory of Sergeant Jack Ridgeway from my early days in the cadets. His claim to fame during these simple little days was a basin haircut, a style adopted by the American Marines and strangely to the present day as a fashion statement. He conducted himself in the manner depicting this cartoon image hairstyle, as one might expect. But from his early beginnings at the training school, he rose through the ranks and became a Detective Superintendent. He was one of the old guard who knew all the twists and turns of police work. Some honest, some more in keeping with the accepted practices in the culture that existed at that time and into the present day with officers from this era.

Of course, Jack was just one of the ever so many throughout the UK who saw such actions as a way of life, a culture perfected through years and honed to suit whatever the requirements. As a consequence Jack was a good detective and well respected, he knew the score. Whilst perhaps not apparent at the time his training school days were a step through the promotion maze. It was the practice in those early days to move promotion prospects through various divisions and departments to give them a wider experience and to ensure that they were experienced officers and consequently, could lead the men under them. More importantly having such a well-grounded level of experience they could adapt as required to protect the men serving under them when 'minor' transgressions came to light. When I say minor, they could be caught with stolen property, they could have battered a prisoner mercilessly, or even taken a day off to go on the piss. However there was also a parallel train of thought with regard to the promotion ladder. Promotion was seen as a reason for moving an individual who had blatantly transgressed and basically abused their position to some form of cosy job they had managed to corner for themselves.

In the private sector such 'transgressions' would be seen as gross misconduct with instant dismissal to follow. The Biggest Gang had different rules and the 'there but for the grace of God' train of thoughts came out to play and any excuse for not taking such drastic action was the order of the day.

It was actually a little like playing promotion roulette as on one day a real detective could be lifted a rank, but sent to training school, the Butlins of the police with a nice 9-to-5 position with plenty of sexual options. What is it about women that they always want to shag the boss? Equally they could be promoted to a real ball-acher such as CID at a shit hole such as Hattersley with no real pubs and certainly no clean women. After all Moors Murderers Ian Brady and Myra Hindley hailed from Hattersley – it is a hovel.

The fact that the trail of the "job's debris" followed the same winding route as the promotion paper trail, caused some confusion and it often wasn't clear with some people if they were actually in the doghouse, or chasing promotion, seeing every move as another rung. There was of course a nucleus of ne'er-do-wells who were so poor at police work, that it was difficult to differentiate between 'in the s…t' or on the ladder and it could certainly not be judged by the new position they were given. There was absolutely no way of telling from wherever they had been moved and for whatever reason and it all proved very confusing. Such a brief summary is probably the only explanation for so many present day Chief Constables of limited experience and expertise.

But back in the 60s and 70s there was an established order both in the force and in general life and a chap called Les Sim was known as Mr Manchester. He was a club owner and operator of the old school and for me he will keep that title as so many pretenders have tried and failed to fill his now deceased shoes. There will always be a diminishing number of us as funerals come and go, a respectful minority who on various get-togethers never fail to mention his name. Then fondly tell anyone of the many stories surrounding this particular legend. He passed away without any real warning around the year 2000 and was cremated at Macclesfield in what was intended to be an anonymous and secret ceremony organized by his effeminate excuse for a son.

It was his intention to tell nobody despite the fact he knew we held his father in such esteem and to get rid of Les as soon as possible with a quick cremation and to move on with his legacy. The 'town' (Manchester) found out and as with so many stories and rumours told everyone and as a result all attended the funeral in some numbers, but at such short notice had not had time to buy the wreaths etc. Some had only found out on the grapevine an hour before, dropped everything and attended. There was a mixture of all Manchester society, the Quality Street Gang with Jack Trickett continuing to deny membership, Roy Garner the smiling assassin, ex-police and all the barmaids who had enjoyed working for Les. With these identifiable individuals were so many other real friends of a less dubious history from his life and all wanted to pay their respects.

The hearse was a heart-breaking sight when it arrived. There was not a flower to be seen, a sad and lonely sight which upset many of us. His son, then the victim of much verbal rumbling, quickly entered the chapel, clearly embarrassed and left in the same way. Les' daughter with whom he had argued merely stood at the cemetery gates. What a dreadful send off. A wake had not been organized after the 10am funeral. Manchester funerals for the characters of the city were well known for the lengths of the wakes and the volume drunk at such gatherings. This could not be permitted and so I contacted a landlord friend of mine, Peter Fancy, who hurriedly put on a breakfast at the Miners Arms in Adlington, near Macclesfield, for all who supported the small function despite knowing none of them. God Bless Les, to absent friends as we all said and raised our glasses.

Whilst the name of Les lingers in my memory two stories come to mind, with things that happened many years earlier when he was still in his heyday though becoming harassed with the petty police attention. Les had had enough of the city. The raids on the clubs were getting more frequent, the quality of the friendly officer was deteriorating and the clientele were generally getting more difficult. It meant he had to employ more doormen, and if the doormen belted anyone, whatever the reason, even if in self defence, the police would arrest the doormen. The licensing rot had set in. Club owners did not know who to trust and there was little point in continually paying the police 'rent' to ensure freedom to serve alcohol well into the early hours. The police were not helping themselves or the public and as a clear result public distrust was growing visibly.

Les upped sticks, left the city centre and took over the Belle Vue Exhibition Centre. This was a massive area of large barn like buildings all adjoined, but with the ability to be divided in the event of smaller promotions. The exhibition centre was part of the Belle Vue Zoo complex. In the good old days it proudly advertised the zoo, which in those days was very impressive but today would be closed down for cruelty because of the standard of the animal accommodation. The Elizabethan Dance Hall promoted regular grab-a-granny nights in addition to all the straight ballroom dancing and as with the Ritz in the city centre any male with all limbs and eyesight could not fail to pull. In the Kings Hall, a seated venue of a circular terraced appearance, they promoted professional wrestling and later as Les moved in professional boxing. They also had a speedway track, which doubled as a venue for stock car racing, an activity I remembered from my childhood when my friends and I would collect pennies from returned lemonade bottles to cover the bus fare and entrance fee. As with the speedway, the greyhound racing track is all that remains of this giant area which is now a housing estate.

Les – God Love him - was never "behind the door" with making a few quid. He arranged a boxing dinner in the

King's Hall and every villain, including myself, attended to show support. I had left the police by then and was operating a very successful private detective agency. I had with me about eight clients from well-known insurance companies. We were drinking in a bar off the main arena and enjoying the evening's sport. Now this one wasn't on the bill, but one of the Pollards, a well-known fighting family, was settling a grudge with another native of God's country, as Salford was popularly known by the 'locals'.

A one-sided fight ensued, coming to an abrupt end when the lovely Mr Pollard rammed the other man's head through a wire reinforced window in the bar door. The victim fell to the floor with a strange squelching sound, probably from blood trapped in his shoes, or the end result of a surprise bowel movement. His ears had attempted to part company with his head and were hanging off at jaunty, casual angles. Blood was pouring out of a multitude of cuts and gashes, most caused by the wire reinforced window in the door, but enhanced by several more blows from Mr Pollard. The cuts blended nicely with the rather obvious black eyes, inflicted earlier in the encounter. Our caring host Les arrived on the scene and surveyed all before him with disgust. He stepped over the bleeding mass, which could have been dead for all he cared and exclaimed: "Look what you have done to my fucking door!" Nobody laughed, Les was serious.

My clients, fresh from their protected Wilmslow existences in the leafy stockbroker belt of Cheshire, had never witnessed anything resembling an angry man.

Let alone this unrecognizable mass, direct from a Quatermass experiment. They were clearly bordering on physical illness, but as everyone else in the bar, attempted to make light of the episode we simply carried on drinking and ignored the situation. Of course if they were in eyesight of Les, they attempted to feign real concern at the damage he had suffered and looked very concerned. The mood was lightened with the handing over of a bundle of bloodied readies from the blood-stained back pocket of the unfortunate victim before the ambulance took the bleeding mass away and Les had the opportunity to examine the floor and proclaim: "Where's Pollard? I want him to see how lucky he has been. Just think if this hadn't been lino, it would have cost him a carpet as well. Blood doesn't come out. He should know. He has spilt enough over the years. "

The massive exhibition halls were not used during certain times of the year and would have remained empty if Les hadn't rented them out for elephant storage to the King's Hall travelling circus. The space was enormous. The trainers, minders and circus labourers all lived in caravans cosily parked inside the cavernous halls. It is not widely known that elephants are very clean and somewhat OCD (Obsessive-Compulsive Disorder) with their toilet practices. Granted, they leave an enormous pile, but even that is tidy. Actually, in the wild they wipe their arse on the nearest tree. But trees were not in abundance in the Belle Vue Conference Centre. Walls on the other hand were all around, literally. The whitewashed walls contrasted well with yard-long skid marks. The elephants moved on with spring to outdoor circus venues. Once the elephant tenants were removed to complete their travels, the walls were whitewashed by Les' army of unemployed, 'bunged' a couple of quid and very soon, again looked perfect. All the doors were left open to air this massive area and get rid of the smell of fresh paint.

All was perfect for the first exhibition of the year. On this occasion it was the Caravan Club get together and sales exhibition. In saving a substantial few quid, Les had tried to leave the central heating switched off because the bill was enormous in the belief that the lighting and body heat from these outdoor types would raise the temperature sufficiently. The vagaries of yet another British Spring Time, however, took over and a cold spell descended, causing more than a few complaints from the now fragile and temperature-sensitive, shivering outdoor types. The central heating quickly and efficiently passed through all the halls and in doing so loosened the lingering skid marks under the lovely new whitewash and with it came the smell permeating from the walls having been generated by a small army of very 'regular' elephants. Of course Les knew that if you can't get blood out of a carpet, you surely couldn't get the smell of elephant shit out of a breeze block wall, however many coats of whitewash. By the end of the day the place smelt like a jungle oasis with the herd returning. Of course, Les immediately knew what the smell was and could even see slight traces of particularly heavy skid marks as the breeze block appeared to relax with the warmth. Les was able to blame the horrendous aroma on a wind change and the compost heap left at the rear by the circus. Ever the entrepreneur Les, didn't look this gift elephant in the mouth, or arse for that matter and immediately started selling the mountain of shite as top of the range compost. 'Imagine Mrs how your roses will come on with elephant turd instead of horse crap, or cow manure on them?' Les was to Gardener's World what Adolf Hitler was to a barmitzvah.

Yet another well-planned use of the Exhibition Centre was for the Lambretta Association. This little get-together appealed to Les. Motor scooters were very popular at this time. Les knew nothing about them and visualized hundreds of harmless scooter riding old ladies, elderly gentlemen, nurses and the like, as he put it rolling up for a bit of bingo. The actual party could not have been further from that imagined and in fact consisted of Mods and all that went with them. They skidded about the halls having built a circuit and ramps. They had a large bonfire outside, which shattered the concrete and which was built from all the, what they saw as, spare wood in the place. Clearly some of this had a considerable value and was necessary for forthcoming exhibitions and attractions. They even built additional ramps on each side of the fire and were holding jumping contests.

The activities of this rampaging horde did not stop at Belle Vue and on leaving the site they broke into every possible shop on Hyde Road. Being a main arterial road on the East of the city, it had many shops. The local pubs were not amused either and whilst they were generally frequented by hard men the constant fighting became a bore. In fact, the only nice thing about them was their haircuts and general dress sense beneath their Parker overcoats. Feigning complete innocence Les bleated that he could not understand why he was hauled into the local Divisional Headquarters and was even accused of assisting this mini-crimewave. Les already had a reputation from the city of taking a fancy to the odd container load and therefore the contents of a multitude of shops would have had immediate appeal. The truth is that Les honestly believed the nurses and old lady script. The police didn't, but what could they do.

With these glory days of fun and frolics firmly in the forefront of my mind, the mishap with the dying declaration and the ensuing investigation was not amusing at all. The death in Didsbury was to cast a terrible shadow over my life and ultimately lead to a change of career and direction. I was exhausted I suppose with the game we were all playing after 13 years, but before I took the decision to depart my public service I was set for one last adventure. Once again it would be out of uniform and once more it would offer even more unbelievable opportunities for ill-gotten gains than anyone could ever imagine.

I certainly had no idea what a wonderful episode in my police career I was letting myself in for when Charlie Horan summoned me to his office after a little incident in Oldham. As I've already mentioned he was a real policeman and grasped the situation immediately when my family were threatened by relatives of the deceased junkie with the purple pants. When that heavy visited the deceased's family and blasted the living room ceiling I got summoned to Charlie's office and was asked what was going on?

As previously mentioned I told Charlie the truth. I had no idea this was going to happen nor who would pull off such a stunt, though I was extremely grateful to whoever it was. Charlie let a glimmer of a smile cross his face as he told me: "I can't have this Dodge City behaviour. You will get into serious trouble. I want you to calm down and leave Didsbury. Go to the Regional Crime Squad. Don't do anything. Sit back and just calm down."

And so a final fresh police adventure was to begin and I really thought at this point that I had seen it all.

Regional crime squad

The Regional Crime Squad was like the Sweeney of Scotland Yard fame. It was a group of very experienced detectives dealing with very experienced criminals. The fact that the entire staff consisted of detectives with years of experience meant that all the elements of extracurricular activities were exaggerated, larger risks and larger rewards were the result for the officers concerned and to service this 'industry' very experienced informants were promised large sums of money for real information on serious crime.

Informants were known as 'snouts' by the police and 'grasses' by the criminal fraternity. Informants came in a variety of guises. There were the petty thieves who looked on it as an extra means of income and who, in the main, would 'shop' their own grandmother. At the opposite end of the 'snout' spectrum were the professional criminals who would happily throw in an underling for a reasonable crime just to be allowed to continue with their own criminal activities as in return a 'blind eye' was turned to allow such activity. This was not a charitable gesture and proceeds from any 'permitted' crime were expected to be shared. In the Drug Squad, I had the informant I have already mentioned and the results were startling. It was the way of the 'police' world at this time, true Life On Mars, but nowadays such pardons are regarded as criminal conspiracies and today, as a result, the next best thing to anarchy reigns. Nobody trusts informants and they in turn do not trust the police and the wheels of justice are grinding to a halt. No one takes any real chances.

We had information via one such informant that a bank was to be robbed at closing time in Withington. We examined the location and "plotted" what observation points we would use and how we could react once the robbery took place. It was all planned and we believed that no firearms would be used by the villains. The day arrived, the day passed and we were in position well before the bank's closing time. I sat in the rear of an innocuous looking builder's van clutching a pickaxe handle and was expected to use it. We saw one of the suspects arrive, look about the area, pay no particular attention to our van and casually drive away. He did not return and clearly had no intention of committing the robbery. We repeated the exercise, based on refreshed information the following Friday, but again the robbery never came off. There was of course always the probability that the 'robbers' were getting information themselves from an RCS officer and merely visited the area to check out his information.

On paper, the Regional Crime Squad had done its duty, the result was negative. There were no crimes to write up, or statements to make and the work for the day had been done. The fact it never came off, didn't seem to concern anyone. Some weeks later the same suspect was arrested 'in possession' of a firearm, duly tried and sentenced to a lengthy term of imprisonment. He protested his innocence throughout, claimed to have been 'planted,' but was never believed. There was never any doubt that this particular person was a very active and dangerous criminal and, as a result, had to be taken from society, which indeed he was. The older villains of this period in the 70s recognized the philosophy of 'it's your turn' and, whilst they screamed a bit, deep down knew there were many incidents they had never been charged with. If you can't stand the heat, don't go into the kitchen as I often say.

Bank robberies were popular, the security was not as today and it was a simple matter to vault what was loosely described as security screens. Again based on 'faultless information' we observed yet another bank in the city on another occasion and this time it was to be from the inside. We had armed officers behind the counter and sat behind desks in the open plan area of the main banking hall. We were all armed and there were police dogs in a rear office. The bank operated as normal with the public coming and going. I was dispensing financial advice which might have led to someone's bankruptcy until a member of the bank staff realized the joke.

Once again nothing happened, at the planned time. Then the informant phoned. The villains had called it off, one of the gang had a hangover and they couldn't get him out of bed. Off we went again, a full day's work done and dusted and on the piss in the city. Everybody knew somebody with a liquor license in the centre and as we split up into smaller groups. We knew we were all guaranteed free lunch and a few free beers.

This boring nonsense continued with the occasional, informant-based arrest, but usually with innumerable visits to innumerable pubs in the city. I wondered some four months down the line if anybody was ever arrested through honest police work, if there is such a thing and was all action really based on dubious informants.

I was still doing my repossessions and making a few quid. It was easier in the RCS and now I didn't have to wait for my days off. I just explained my absence with visiting an informant in say Liverpool, if that was where the car was and off I went.

The suicide scenario and accusations of murder still bothered me. I could not settle any more in a job which couldn't protect me, which would use an office boy to investigate me, and which had no appreciation of the risks we all took at the pointed end. My family could have been killed and they were trying to prosecute me, or at least go through the very concerning motions. They'd have had no qualms about putting me in the dock if Coyle had managed to put together a case, but he wasn't exactly a genius on the detecting front, or any other front for that matter.

I was really pissed off; I was earning more money with the repossessions than my police salary. Finally I submitted my resignation. It is a common belief in some areas of the police and the trickier regions of Manchester, especially the Commercial Hotel on

Liverpool Road and of course the Mecca of all Manchester gossip, the Sir Ralph Abercrombie a pub immediately next to Bootle Street Police Station, once filled with pissed-up officers of all ranks and standing before their tour of duty. The gossip was that I was sacked, told to resign, or something similar. I just resigned, I had had enough. Charlie Horan tried to talk me out of it. He was excellent. The Chief Constable of the time whose name escapes me, not Anderton, also suggested I should reconsider. Charlie Horan said I could have a quiet life until I settled down, by which I suppose he meant, just do nothing like most of the RCS.

Fortunately, I didn't take his advice and as I see the police as it is today, I realize that I made the correct decision. Police were no longer permitted to drink in the 'Abercrombie' and it eventually closed only to be reopened by a 'headhunted' George of The Circus fame. If the force was run by the Charlie Horans, the Tom Butchers, Eric Jones and the rest, it would have been a different ending. It was not then and certainly is not today. The days of accelerated promotion, university graduates and examination professionals were upon us. There was now no place for the real detective or uniformed constable for that matter.

I worked a few more weeks. I had no faith in the leadership or the protection I could be offered and took all my owed days off and holidays. I was out of the police. And I felt very empty. For a few weeks after, I still went into the Royal Oak believing I could continue with the same social relationships I had enjoyed for so many years, but the atmosphere was frosty even from people

I liked and trusted. A Chief Inspector known as "Strange," a bald headed pompous arse, warned the lads not to help me with information and have nothing to do with my private detective activities having failed miserably for so long to detect my activities himself.

As I look back, all the bad was for a purpose. It all came good in the end. It is the processing that is important, being able to make good of the bad somehow. Life tends to do that, if we let it. I found my way. It was a start and I found my way. I left the police to go into a business and eventually it made me a rich man, a millionaire with the largest private detective agency of its type, specializing only in surveillance without all the minor support services, possibly anywhere in the world.

The fact I was aiming to become a self-made millionaire from the humble beginnings of my childhood was something the police in general could not accept and I was constantly in their sights and accused of associations with all manner of criminal activities. They were basically jealous. There was a defined culture in the police where everyone moaned, they saw the 'grass as greener' out of the police, but didn't have the balls to leave. I on the other hand thought 'bollocks to it' and made the switch.

It remains a move I am very happy with though. My third book will tell all about my life as a Private Eye or Private Dick as some might say. But before then I'll outline the first bit of revenge the police took on me by fitting me up for a fall. In the words of Chumbawamba: 'I get knocked down and I get up again you ain't never going to keep me down.'

With thanks to Chumbawamba for a soundtrack to survival and who can forget their lead singer Danbert Nobacon pouring that jug of water over the head of Deputy Prime Minister John Prescott at the 1998 Brit Awards.

Now that's a band awash with talent and old Two Jags certainly deserved his drenching. I've always found him a bit of a wet lettuce and now out of the political limelight he hangs on to notoriety with stupid attacks, generally in goobledegook, on ridiculous subjects.

Into the Big Wide World Without Insurance

It didn't take long at all before I was becoming well known as a private detective and, as a survivor of the 60s and 70s Life On Mars mode of rough, tough policing, I was known to bend the rules and get the information and arrests if required. I was known to be fair, not too fair, and always open to negotiation. We all helped each other in the CID. If anyone had a friend, whether a villain or not, if they vouched for them then they were okay and negotiations would take place. It may have been a pal, locked up with a bit of stolen property. A bit being either a pile of scrap metal, or a container full of hairdryers, or other such half-inched electrical goods and the value did not matter, it was the principal of: 'You scratch my back and I'll scratch yours.'

Of course the size of the 'product' meant extra effort if it was substantial and to write off a container as found property always required a certain level of expertise. The Hillsborough conspiracy was born of this practice that showed how simple it was to account for any situation. To write off 96 deaths involved the same basic principal as writing off a container. Even with the contents removed, the container had a value, an owner and an interested insurance company. The theft of containers was rife and many individuals preferred to not involve the insurance company and deal with any reward direct, thereby saving on the next year's premium. Containers were practically indestructible and yet just disappeared, probably sent to Russia full of stolen cars and never to be seen again.

It was simpler for the property owner to pay for the return of the container and then have a convenient fire to account for the loss of the contents. The detective acted as the middle man and convinced the owner to pay the informant, who knew the whereabouts and wished to remain anonymous. The helpful detective was handed the readies, a realistic proportion was skimmed and all shared out amongst the various officers. Of course there was no informant other than the individual who was arrested for the handling. No container, no charge and a further commission more as a fine to the officers, as the hairdryers were sold.

The local criminal fraternity was fully aware of all the working practices and with these in mind I was approached by a motor trader, who had been arrested for tampering with the mileage on a considerable number of motor cars. This was fondly known as "clocking" and he was good at it. This was not a matter to be tidied up. This was a motor trader, an occupation notorious for their gossiping, caught red-handed with clocked cars and no real excuse. He knew he was in the shit. He had clocked about 30 cars. Motor traders always associated with each other and developed a close working relationship and whilst whatever stock they had was their own it appeared from the outside that they were all concerned together.

My trader had friends who were caught in the same 'net' and had actually clocked more than 300 cars, some of them actually with changed identities having been previously stolen. This tricky little bastard was rightfully concerned as to whether the Stolen Car Squad was intending to link him with "his friends" and in doing so plant a little documentation to link names and a few well-chosen verbals when under arrest. Such a connection, however innocent, could easily be adapted to a criminal conspiracy to defraud the innocent car-buying public. This was an offence which was actually easier to prove and was a much more serious charge with a greater sentence than the one he was facing.

The beauty of such a charge was that it was also a recognized and well-tested means of getting a conviction where evidence is sparse and works on the principal: 'If you throw enough shit at a wall, some will stick.' The evidence is all encompassing and deliberately complicated in that many cars would be identified and some of the names were associated with them. In addition a few of the same names with others not already mentioned would be associated with a different group of arrested dealers. It was a favourite practice at court to produce a 'spider's web' of a chart, naming names and cars with complicated lines connecting various groups and cars. The fact that some of the dealers did not know everyone, or had never seen the majority of cars was not an issue.

Additional charges were also directed at certain individuals or a separate group and always the charges were lesser and deliberately thrown in, often based on total fiction to attract the accused to plead guilty to a lower offence, which they invariably did. What commenced as a massive conspiracy to defraud was dramatically reduced out of all recognition, producing guilty pleas which themselves were a crime detection in addition to all the other charted matters which were then shown as TICs giving a tidy end result with a lump out of the recorded crime rate into the bargain. Clearly my tricky little friend knew all the angles and whatever the outcome he was probably looking at another term with Her Majesty's Prison Service which was an occupational hazard he had endured for years.

I knew an officer in the Stolen Vehicle Squad and had served with him in uniform at Bootle Street. Our wives had worked together at a bank in the city and the two of us had regularly taken cocktails in the town on our searches for a bit on the side. With such a history and a pedigree of handling a few suspect items himself, I was confident he would assist me. Strangely I wasn't asking him to do anything illegal. I just wanted some information which would have been known later, in any case. We arranged to meet in a pub, close to the station where he served and also close to the office, so close we often had a steak and a sherry as it was a Berni Inn – the height of fashion in those days.

These were without doubt the best steaks in town at this time and a couple of schooners were all in the cheap meal deal. I had a pal at the time who worked for the now defunct News of the World – the top selling tabloid Sunday newspaper of the day. This chap was a big friend of the legendary Manchester United footballer George Best and would often be given the job of substitute on dates if the Manchester striker had scored elsewhere. This particular night a famous actress from an established acting dynasty was being given the elbow by gorgeous

George and my friend had the not unpleasant job of wining and dining the snubbed star and breaking the news. A legover afterwards was also on the horizon if everything went well and we're still not far out of the swinging 60s here, so sex as dessert after a fine steak was often on the menu.

This particular evening though it all went a bit pear-shaped. My chum had had a couple of pints before the date had got underway and in his own inimitable fashion had begun to charm the famous actress out of her underwear – at least in his own mind he had. All was going swimmingly as the fine red flowed along with the beer when suddenly the call of nature took hold. Excusing himself from the table my friend stood up, completely forgetting he'd tucked the tablecloth into his trousers as a sort of super-size serviette. As soon as he stood, the ale, the red, the glasses, the steaks and mushy vegetables all spilled across the table into the lap of the attractive actress in a veritable tsunami of wine, beer and food. It wasn't the best way to get a girl's pants off and she swiftly made her excuses and left. Taking them off on her own the moment she stepped through the door of her hotel room.

Many years later, about three decades or so to be precise, my pal was interviewing a younger member of the same acting dynasty who was starring in some TV show or other. Being fearless in his pursuit of the truth and keen to recount his former famous date my pal mentions the relative's name and the magical words Berni Inn and immediately the young actress started to titter and replied: 'Fantastic, you're tablecloth man.'

A legend in theatrical circles ever since – my friend still dines out on this story, though these days he doesn't tuck the tablecloth into his trousers.

Anyway I digress, back then on my Berni Inn date with my old officer pal it was Monday teatime and the small cocktail bar adjoining the restaurant area was strangely busy for the time of day. Innocently, I discussed the predicament that my trader pal was in and that he was concerned that he would be 'cocked up' for a conspiracy, when everyone knew he worked alone, or more to the point that he was such a bent little bastard that no one trusted him with their money.

My former colleague and close chum was fully aware that I would be earning now that I was in the big wide world and just as a matter of fact with no reluctance at all, he asked: "What is in it for me?" I knew how much I was to be paid, so I was happy to offer him £50 even though I'd rather have just bought him a few pints for the information and a fine meal. I had just completed 13 years in the police, I had learnt all the tricks and indeed I had personally had many such conversations with colleagues and friends, not all in the police and 'little earners' were always the order of the day. This was never seen as a bribe and indeed in this case really wasn't by the usual standards of accepted practice. It was just a bit of banditry and you have to remember it was a way of life.

Without a word, we knew what we were doing, we were repeating actions we had done so many times. Words were not required and as I said, this was accepted practice. In unison we just turned and entered the gents' toilets, away from the public gaze, where I counted out the readies which I handed to him and placed in his sweaty out stretched hand. We returned to the bar, recalling a shagging expedition of some years earlier when all hell broke loose.

And at that very moment the entire drinking populace of the pub jumped to their feet, pulled out their warrant cards and I was arrested. At first I was sure it was a Jeremy Beadle type stunt, but no and unbelievably my 'good friend' had shopped me. He was wearing a "wire" and I just couldn't believe it, still cannot comprehend it to this day as this was standard practice. This was a man I had known for years, we had shagged together, our wives worked together and he had asked for money. Rather than just say no, I decided to help him out with the readies, as I knew a policeman's wage was not enough to enjoy the shagging he so loved and in return for my misguided kindness I was now under arrest. Premeditated, deliberate and very shitty that is how I'd describe his behaviour. This was the Biggest Gang ganging up on me.

To be fair Hoagy Carmichael my DS during my Drug Squad days phoned me to meet up. By then I didn't know who to trust and refused. Perhaps, in the cold light of day all I had to do was pay the 'fine' and move on.

From the contrived evidence I was charged with attempting to bribe a police officer. There was no attempt he nearly snatched my hand off. After several seething months I eventually, appeared at Manchester

Crown Court. With my knowledge I knew I could have pleaded not guilty. There was so much evidence going for me, but all circumstantial on my part. The end result was that I had bunged the officer. He had a note which was a consecutive number with others I held in my pocket. It was a gamble, in those days everyone believed the police and juries were rarely swayed. I still felt I would probably have got away with it.

However, I was promised a deal from the prosecution barrister that if I pleaded guilty, I would not be sent to prison. The judge had agreed this. I had too many commitments, both work and family as I had two babies, all the usual overheads and the need to pay the mortgage. I took the deal. It meant nothing at the time I was a 'big boy' and it seemed so simple. Yet as my business grew the guilty plea proved to be, not such a good idea, and was on my shoulder casting a shadow over everything I did. I was becoming very successful in my business and with the success came a certain level of fame and column inches in local and national newspapers even the glossy magazine Cheshire Life, wow the pinnacle of success.

This notoriety proved to be the biggest fine ever. I had a criminal conviction and as a consequence, in the eyes of the law, was totally discredited. I could not give evidence on oath, I was a criminal and barristers, judges and newspapers could say so in whatever terms they wished. The Manchester Evening News regularly featured me and always mentioned the criminal record and it continued until a new editor agreed with my solicitor that the same old stories about me were no longer in the public interest.

The fact that I was unable to give evidence in any court for fear of "damaged reputation" being used against me meant that I could no longer become involved in investigations, which may have resulted in my having to give evidence in court. Again it was a case of one law for the 'Job' and one law for Joe Public.

This arrest has remained with me ever since and the bitterness has never faded. That is despite the fact that I introduced women to the wife of the 'friend' who arrested me as his girlfriends. She was very ill at the time, but I just did not care. Other incidents which will remain under wraps continued until he transferred to a force on the South coast to serve with his brother. Fate moves in a strange manner and whilst in Puerto Banus, Marbella, on a friend's yacht I met his Chief Constable over a drink. He was old school and being entertained by a local businessman from his force. He was interested as I related my tale and highlighted a few less than honest episodes when we worked together. I am told his career took an unfortunate turn thereafter and for several years I continued to receive a Christmas card from my lofty pal.

I've other Chief Constable stories to impart, my links to the John Stalker investigation into the Government's Shoot To Kill Policy and I'll get round to detailing how I became a multi-millionaire.

My journey has been a revelation, mostly to me on occasions, as I recall the remarkable route from a rented house on a police probationer's salary to a mansion home with a serious wedge in the bank. I've even had Hollywood come calling, or at least Huddersfield – where some Yorkshire movie makers with big budget film finance backing are keen to transform my story to the silver screen. I am very much looking forward to the casting couch chapters that will with luck make their way into the third book of my trilogy.

I've not finished yet, not by a long way and perhaps Frank Sinatra's 'My Way' might be the melody to accompany my private detective days. I'll just put that on the I-Pod and start tapping the keyboard. I am chortling now as I think of some of the outrageous things we got up to during my spell as a Manchester celebrity. Appearing on TV both locally and nationally as a recognized expert on all things to do with surveillance and the private detective field and I know book three will be full of fun and some very famous names indeed.

In addition to TV personalities, soccer managers and other noted individuals I will be mentioning others who regard themselves as personalities in the arena of private detective work. All trained by me and all who owe me everything, so now I'll highlight their dishonesty and their abuse of clients. These are clients who chose to trust their abilities, despite the varying levels of evidential dishonesty they regard as normal working practices. And I am not just talking about hacking and blagging.

Of course, I once again swear to tell the truth, the whole truth and nothing but the truth. A few former colleagues should now be quaking in their boots, but I can confirm I will certainly be naming the guilty parties at every possible opportunity. Onwards and upwards towards the end of my trilogy and I am looking forward to the next chapter in my life already.

THE END

www.ingramcontent.com/pod-product-compliance
Lightning Source LLC
LaVergne TN
LVHW091249080426
835510LV00007B/180